Arp in his studio at Meudon, 1958. Photo André Villers

The Museum of Modern Art, New York

edited with an introduction by James Thrall Soby

articles by Jean Hans Arp, Richard Huelsenbeck, Robert Melville,

Carola Giedion-Welcker

distributed by Doubleday & Company, Inc., Garden City, New York

CONTENTS

ACKNOWLEDGMENTS

The artist himself and Marguerite Hagenbach have been of constant and immense help in the preparation of this book and the exhibition it describes. I should also like to thank Jean Arp for writing the fine article which appears in these pages; I am indebted, too, to Richard Huelsenbeck, Robert Melville, and Carola Giedion-Welcker for their important texts. Arp's article was translated from the German by Ralph Manheim; Carola Giedion-Welcker's text was translated by Christl Ritter and Eleanor C. Munro.

I am grateful to Alfred H. Barr, Jr., for his valuable editorial suggestions; to Sidney Janis, Arp's present American dealer, for his patient assistance; to Jane Wade for making available the files of the late Curt Valentin's gallery, with which she was associated.

When this publication was begun, Sam Hunter was Associate Curator of the Museum's Department of Painting and Sculpture. He worked tirelessly in assembling data about Arp and his works, and was greatly helped by Alicia Legg of the same Department. The book was seen through the press with her usual amiable efficiency by Frances Pernas of the Museum's Publications Department, and was designed by Charles Oscar.

J. T. S.

TRUSTEES OF THE MUSEUM OF MODERN ART

INTRODUCTION: THE SEARCH FOR NEW FORMS

"A one-man laboratory for the discovery of new form," Alfred Barr once called Jean (Hans) Arp. The description seems accurate when one considers the variety of Arp's plastic innovations in many media. At seventy-one his freshness of vision remains undiminished, and he works with the enthusiasm and boldness of his earlier career, creating sculptures in the round, bas reliefs and those thoroughly original two-dimensional images which have extended in an important direction the vocabulary of art in our time.

To a number of his works Arp has applied the title, "objects arranged according to the laws of chance," and there can be no doubt that the occasional miracles of accident have had particular meaning for him, as when he makes his string compositions, his *papiers déchirés* and his automatic drawings. His alertness to subconscious sources of inspiration is swift and apparently inexhaustible, a fact which once attracted him, though briefly, to the surrealist movement. Whatever he touches carries the mark of strong personality and estimable skill. One assumes that he considers spontaneity a primary asset of art. What cannot easily be explained is how he retains this spontaneity when reworking some of his sculptures in varying dimensions and materials, so that each version has the look of new wonder.

The automatism of many of Arp's works has tended to obscure the importance of his capacity for acute observation in viewing the tangible world around him. The truth is that he is among other things a naturalist of the very finest order, stripping human and animal forms to a magic essence that far transcends realism to arrive at subtle evocation. Consider, for example, the allusive cogency of the *Owl's Dream* (page 87), wherein the silent bird is wreathed in sleep. Or consider the swelling, slithering vitality of his *Snake Movement II* (page 108), epitomizing the coiling of serpents. The word "abstract" becomes almost meaningless when applied to some of Arp's sculptures, though the discipline of abstraction has engaged him persistently, notably in his many brilliant *collages*. And it must be added that Arp is one of the few contemporary artists whose contribution to psychological explorations has been just as important as his contribution to problems of formal order.

Arp was born in Strasbourg on September 16, 1887. Extremely precocious, he drew at a very early age. But then, as he recounts in the following pages, he tired of "the everlasting copying of stuffed birds and withered flowers," and turned to poetry for relief, leaving the Strasbourg School of Applied Art to read avidly the German Romantic, Clemens Brentano, and the poetry of the members

Moustache Hat. c. 1918. Lithograph, 10¾ x 13". The Museum of Modern Art, New York, gift of J. B. Neumann

of the *Sturmer* group. In 1904 he was exposed to modern painting on a visit to Paris, and within a few years again became an art student, first at the Weimar Art School, later (1908) at the Académie Julian in Paris. His rare visual sensitivity made it possible for him to appreciate the more advanced aspects of Parisian art even in youth, and by 1911 he had organized with friends an exhibition at Lucerne, under the title *Moderne Bund,* which showed works by Gauguin, Hodler, Matisse, Picasso, Arp himself, and others today less eminent. The same year he visited Kandinsky, came into contact with the artists of the famous *Blaue Reiter,* and soon was contributing to their exhibitions and to the publication bearing the group's name.

By the time he was twenty-five Arp had emerged as a poet and a painter of marked distinction. The dual role, which Arp has continued to play to this day, has its pitfalls, and we are all aware of its debilitating effect on the lesser members of the Romantic movement in both France and Germany, the two countries which between them supply Arp's intellectual patrimony as an Alsatian. But Arp, unlike the Romantics, has never confused or over-stepped the boundaries which separate literature from the fine arts. His writings and his visual works have a comparable intensity and richness of analogy, yet each is faithful to its own identity and neither pre-empts the function of the other. For how many other leading painters and sculptors of our day can we claim so decided and intrinsic a literary talent?

In 1915, according to his remarkable text in this book, Arp created his first "essential" picture. He adds that he was playing with children's blocks at the time. The statement will sound weird and even frivolous to those puritans for whom art is a matter of unyielding solemnity. But it characterizes Arp's profound interest in simple objects. "My 'first successful picture,'" he says, "grew out of this playing and building with elementary forms." Throughout his career Arp has been nourished by plain objects which could never have potential meaning in the creative sense for artists of less lively imaginative powers. Moustaches, forks, navels, eggs, leaves, clouds, birds, shirt fronts — these and other commonplace components of the tangible world have inspired him continuously to achieve an art in which iconography is rid of all storytelling purpose and from which an invaluable new visual order emerges.

One might say that Arp's regard for everyday objects is essentially metaphysical and that his aim is to restore to these objects their preternatural mystery. In this connection his art may be compared with some profit to that of the Surrealists who, following the example of Giorgio de Chirico, have disrupted the logic of ordinary associations by combining in their pictures objects of totally disparate meaning, so as to arrive at a provocative, new and unforeseen scenario derived from subconscious dictation. The difference, however, is obvious. Arp does not admire incongruity for its shock value. Rather his aim is to give a penetrating

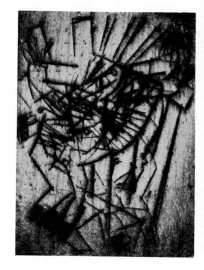

Crucifixion. 1914. Engraving, 4½ x 3½". Collection Lucien Lefebvre-Foinet, Paris

dignity to familiar forms, both animate and inanimate, through a reappraisal of their metabolic capacity. Similarly, the "double image," a persistent surrealist device for obviating reality, has seldom if ever interested him. His statements about reality are unequivocal on the surface, but they revive a long-buried archaeology of the human spirit to which many other artists have since turned with profit and to which many more undoubtedly will turn in the future.

In 1914 Arp lived in Paris, where he became the friend of Picasso, Apollinaire, Max Jacob, Modigliani, Delaunay, and other leaders of the modern movement in the arts. The following year he moved to Zurich, and exhibited his first mature *collages* and tapestries. His interest in these two media is typical. The first, invented by Picasso and Braque only a few years before, had the appeal of a revolutionary departure from the authority of the hand-painted oil; the second had descended over the centuries from a position of august skill and eloquence to one of academic handicraft. Arp must have liked the challenge inherent in both. There followed the superb group of *collages*, tapestries, and fabrics through which he won a more and more influential following. His revolutionary fervor found support and encouragement when he joined Hugo Ball, Emmy Hennings, Richard Huelsenbeck, Marcel Janco, and Tristan Tzara in founding Zurich's Dada movement. At this time, too, he met Sophie Taeuber, who became his wife and with whom he often collaborated on works of art, one of his cherished beliefs being that creative activity should be a shared rather than a solitary process.

In 1916 and 1917 Arp produced the first of those painted wood reliefs to which he has since turned his attention consistently. The authority of his very first reliefs such as the *Portrait of Tzara*, the *Forest*, and *Plant Hammer* (pages 19, 35, 36) is remarkable, and within a few years he had progressed to works as supremely inventive as the *Birds in an Aquarium*, *Shirt Front and Fork* and *Plate, Fork, and Navel* (pages 38, 41). By then he had been active in the Dada movements of Cologne, Berlin, and other Central European cities. He had also become the friend of Kurt Schwitters and, above all, of Max Ernst, with whom he collaborated in painting a series of "Fatagaga" pictures — "guaranteed to be gasometric." The playfulness and insolence of the Dada movement obviously appealed to him, yet it did nothing to contaminate his unflinching integrity as an artist. As the Dada movement waned he gravitated with many of his colleagues toward Surrealism, and in 1925 took part in the first group exhibition of the surrealist artists at the Galerie Pierre in Paris.

The 1920s were especially fertile years for Arp and during that decade he finished many of his beguiling string compositions (pages 40, 50, 51) and some of his finest wooden reliefs, among them the *Shirt and Tie*, *Arranged According to the Laws of Chance*, and *Two Heads* (pages 48, 49, 53). Yet during the 1930s he was to broaden his expressive range still further. At this time, disgusted with the fading neatness of his earlier *collages*, as he recounts later in these pages, he

9

began to produce his torn-paper drawings, impetuously and often with violence. He continued to make wooden reliefs, of course. But sculpture in the round interested him more and more. We see him moving toward it in the *Hand Fruit* of 1930 (page 54), one of the earliest of his free-standing pieces.

By 1931 Arp had progressed to the *Bell and Navels* (page 55), still executed in wood, his favorite material up to that point. In 1932, however, he began to produce his sculptures in bronze and various kinds of stone, the latter, of course, being mostly carved pieces. That same year he joined the *Abstraction-Création* group on whose other members his influence was considerable. He was then often interested, as was Henry Moore a few years later, in assembling several independently executed sculptural forms within a given work of art, as in *Human Concretion on Oval Bowl* (page 63), and in *To Be Lost in the Woods* (page 55) whose pedestal is as thoughtfully conceived as the object it sustains.

It must be added that Arp, whose early (1916–18) *collages* had been concerned with geometric shapes, particularly squares and rectangles, had long since become a leading and persuasive advocate of the biomorphic and had written his celebrated dictum, "Art is a fruit that grows in man, like a fruit on a plant, or a child in its mother's womb." As this advocate, he has had a deep effect on artists slightly younger than himself such as Moore and Calder and, quite possibly, Miró, though Arp with characteristic modesty feels that the last-named, who lived in the same building as he at number 22, rue Tourlaque, Montmartre, during the years 1925 and 1926, arrived at his mature vision by quite another route. Moreover, Arp's influence on the arts of design, not excluding architecture, has been of vast importance. He as much as anyone brought about the revolt against the geometric preoccupations of a great number of preceding artists from the cubists to Mondrian. The shift in his own direction is glaringly apparent if we compare his *Rectangles Arranged According to the Laws of Chance* of 1916 (page 35) with such a work as *Color Tear* of 1947 or *Bird and Necktie* of 1954 (pages 83, 104).

By the middle and later 1930s Arp had reached his full stature as a sculptor in the round, creating such masterworks as the *Human Concretion* in cast stone, the *Stone Formed by the Human Hand* in Jura limestone, the *Shell Crystal* in granite and the *Homage to Rodin* in granite (pages 65, 71, 73, 68). The last-named piece is a touching reminder that Rodin's significance was not lost on his heirs in sculpture even during those years when professional art historians and critics tended to find his work too grandiose and dramatic. It may be, too, that Rodin's mastery of bronze surfaces led Arp to use this hardy, traditional material more and more often. One must add as a matter of personal opinion that Arp usually seems more at ease with stone than with bronze, possibly for the very reason that the former is a more "natural" material. It is no accident that one of the sculptures mentioned above is entitled *Stone Formed by the Human Hand*. In many of Arp's recent stone sculptures, whether cast or carved,

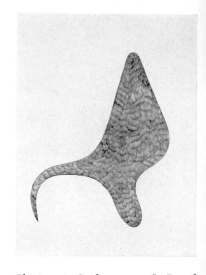

Planimetric Sculpture. 1958. Pencil, 27½ x 19¾". Collection the artist

10

there is an intimacy between artist and material which metal sometimes obscures.

During the Second World War Arp took refuge in Switzerland, where he continued to work in the many media which have made him one of the most versatile of contemporary artists. In 1949 and again in 1950 he came to America and on the second of these journeys completed a monumental wood relief for Harvard University's Graduate Center at Cambridge. His search for new form was and remains unrelenting, and both this relief and the one he executed in metal on cement for Ciudad Universitaria at Caracas, Venezuela, (1956) make clear his knowledgeability in questions of scale. It may be, nevertheless, that his greatest achievement of the past twenty years has been his sculpture in the round. At any rate, outstanding sculptures from his hand have followed one another with admirable profusion: the intensely tactile little *Snake Bread* of 1942 (page 75); the *Chimerical Font* of 1947 (page 85); the almost mystical *Head with Claws* of 1949 (page 86); the exquisite *Configuration in Serpentine Movements* of 1950 (page 97); the frighteningly real *Cobra-Centaur* of 1952 (page 96); *Oru* (page 97); the majestic *Ptolemy* of 1953, with its breath-taking balance of solids and voids (page 100); the enigmatically sensual *Seated,* executed last year (page 110).

Since the Second World War, in addition to his sculptures, bas reliefs, *collages* and drawings, Arp has designed several fine tapestries. His interest in textiles is of very long standing; in 1915 at the Tanner Gallery in Zurich, as briefly noted, he had included in his first important exhibition tapestries and embroidery, partly in protest against what he considered to be the tyranny of oil painting as the preferred medium for serious artists. The range of Arp's technical facility, as noted before, is most impressive. He turns from one form of expression to another with startling rapidity and conviction — from *papiers déchirés* to the recent drawings done with an engraver's precision (opposite), from *collages* to bas reliefs, from woodcuts to paintings, from paintings to sculpture in the round. He gives absolute credence to those falling-stars of inspiration which veer into his artist's consciousness, blazing, sometimes irregular and quite often, one assumes, uninvited.

A word must be said about Arp's emotional and intellectual flexibility. His works may have the solemnity of a sacred oath, and then again he delights in a guffaw, as when he invented his eggboard game (see page 39): "An indefinite number of gladiators open the game in goosestep . . . and deeming themselves the winners, march busily smashing eggs with the eggboard through the goal . . . the use of hardboiled eggs is unfair." At times his absorption in his art is pious; at times he becomes deliciously irreverent, though always within the discipline of a firm creative conscience. Like all fine artists he is never completely predictable. But one thing even now may be foretold with certainty: that Arp's high and unique place in our century's art will remain indisputable.　　　　JAMES THRALL SOBY

LOOKING

To open my eyes, to see, to look, to contemplate the world, to watch clouds and trees, to behold cities and buildings, to look works of art in the eye, to look men in the eye, to see, to look — ever since my childhood this has been my greatest joy. I have seen many magnificent buildings in Switzerland, France, Italy, and Greece. But the most beautiful thing of all is the interior of the Strasbourg cathedral with its great jewels, the miracle of its stained-glass windows. I will write a thousand and one poems about those windows. In 1958, after many years, I revisited Strasbourg, my birthplace. I visited the house where I was born, a Renaissance structure. Here I spent the first years of my life. I clearly remember my consternation, in that house, at my brother's arrival in the world. It was there that I began to draw. But by the time I was sixteen the everlasting copying of stuffed birds and withered flowers at the Strasbourg School of Applied Art not only poisoned drawing for me but destroyed my taste for all artistic activity. I took refuge in poetry. My old love of the German Romantics, Novalis, Brentano, Arnim is still with me. At that time I discovered Rimbaud's *Illuminations* and Maeterlinck's *Serres Chaudes* in a French bookstore, and soon I was surrounded by mountains of books.

From Strasbourg I moved to Switzerland where I lived in great isolation on Lake Lucerne. Gradually I began to draw again. I tried to be "natural," in other words, the exact opposite of what the drawing teachers call "faithful to nature." I made my first experiments with free forms. I looked for new constellations of form such as nature never stops producing. I tried to make forms grow. I put my trust in the example of seeds, stars, clouds, plants, animals, men, and finally in my own innermost being. But later on, in Weimar as well as Paris, the teachers seemed determined to spoil the visible and invisible world for me. They kept trying to make me copy, imitate. But I refused to be confused or led astray, and in 1915 I produced my first "essential" picture. I believe that I was playing with some children's blocks at the time. My "first successful picture" grew out of this playing and building with elementary forms. It contains both the crucifixion and the head of Christ crucified, which form independent pictures within the picture. And I dreamed of pictures that would combine innumerable pictures within them. I might add that forty-three years were to pass before the second figure was discovered in this "first successful picture." What Christopher Columbus did for America, Marguerite Hagenbach did for my "first successful picture." It was she who discovered the head in it.

In 1915 I met Sophie Taeuber and her work encouraged me in constructing

Horses. 1914. Engraving, 9⅞ x 13".
Collection the artist

pictures. Sophie Taeuber was one of the first to construct pictures. It was not until 1919 that we received a few numbers of the Dutch review *De Stijl* and became acquainted with the work of Theo van Doesburg and Piet Mondrian. In the last few years Sophie Taeuber's work has begun to come in for the appreciation it deserves. Dr. Georg Schmidt, the far-sighted director of the Basel museum, called attention to her work many years ago.

In 1914 Marcel Duchamp, Francis Picabia, and Man Ray, then in New York, had created a *dada* (hobby-horse) that left nothing to be desired. But great was their distress, for they found no name for it. And because it was nameless, we in Zurich knew nothing of its existence. But when in 1916 we engendered our Dada and it was born, we — Hugo Ball, Tristan Tzara, Richard Huelsenbeck, Emmy Hennings, Marcel Janco, and I — fell rejoicing into each other's arms and cried out in unison: "Da, da ist ja unser Dada" ("There, there's our Dada"). Dada was against the mechanization of the world. Our African evenings were simply a protest against the rationalization of man. My gouaches, reliefs, plastics were an attempt to teach man what he had forgotten — to dream with his eyes open. Even then I had a foreboding that men would devote themselves more and more furiously to the destruction of the earth. The choicest fruits on the tree of Dada, gems from top to toe, were those raised by my friend Max Ernst and myself in Cologne. A little later we moved to the Tyrol and Tristan Tzara joined us in the good work. In Cologne Max Ernst and I founded the great enterprise of "Fatagaga" under the patronage of the charming Baroness Armanda von Duldge-dalzen and the well-to-do Herr Baargeld (Mr. Cashmoney). Overcome by an irresistible longing for snakes, I created a project for reformed rattlesnakes, beside which the insufferable rattlesnake of the firm of Laocoön and Sons is a mere worm. At the very same moment Max Ernst created "Fata." My reformed rattlesnake firm and Max Ernst's Fata firm were merged under the name of Fatagaga, and can be brought back to life at any time on request. The important thing about Dada, it seems to me, is that the Dadaists despised what is commonly regarded as art, but put the whole universe on the lofty throne of art. We declared that everything that comes into being or is made by man is art. Art can be evil, boring, wild, sweet, dangerous, euphonious, ugly, or a feast to the eyes. The whole earth is art. To draw well is art. Rastelli was a wonderful artist. The nightingale is a great artist. Michelangelo's *Moses:* Bravo! But at the sight of an inspired snow man, the Dadaists also cried bravo.

The building of the Aubette in Strasbourg in 1926 is another milestone in my life. Sophie Taeuber, Theo van Doesburg, the architect and painter, and I, were able, thanks to Messrs. Horn, our far-sighted patrons and their enlightened understanding of art, to carry through one of the first syntheses of architecture, painting and sculpture. The ten rooms, on which we worked for two years, have meanwhile been destroyed by a microcephalic owner, a deed worthy of Hitler.

13

If the Aubette were still standing, it would be one of the most notable sights in Strasbourg, for there is probably nothing like it in modern architecture. One of the destroyed reliefs was reconstructed last year for the university of Caracas, by Villanueva, from Sophie Taeuber's original drawings.

In 1927 Sophie Taeuber and I moved to Meudon in the outskirts of Paris. Gradually, very gradually, the first art dealers in Paris and Brussels began to take an interest in my work. In Switzerland, which I had regularly revisited, I found my most faithful friends, who were also collectors, Mr. and Mrs. Giedion-Welcker, Mr. and Mrs. Hoffmann-Stehlin, Mr. and Mrs. Oscar Müller-Widmann, Mr. and Mrs. Friedrich, and Miss Marguerite Hagenbach. Kurt Schwitters came from Germany to see me and we worked together on his novel, since vanished, *Franz Müllers Drahtfrühling* (*Franz Müller's Wire Springtime*). In 1925 I exhibited at the first surrealist group show and contributed to their magazines. They encouraged me to ferret out the dream, the idea behind my plastic work, and to give it a name. For many years, roughly from the end of 1919 to 1931, I interpreted most of my works. Often the interpretation was more important for me than the work itself. Often it was hard to render the content in rational words. Here are a few of the titles, interpretations, poems of my "dreamed plastic works" of those years: The Eggboard — Paolo and Francesca — Bird Mask — Navel — Navel Bottle — Moon Frog — Mountain, Table, Anchors, Navel — Semicolon — Rhymed Stones — Navel and Two Thoughts — Church Clock — Delivered Flame — Pregnant Amphora — Three Walking Canes — Shadows Enjoying a Black View. These titles were often abbreviated little stories such as this one for "Mountain-Table-Anchors-Navel" in my book *Unser täglicher Traum* (*Our Daily Dream*): "A dreamer can make eggs as big as houses dance, bundle up flashes of lightning, and make an enormous mountain, dreaming of a navel and two anchors, hover over a poor enfeebled table that looks like the mummy of a goat." At that time Theo van Doesburg's magazine *De Stijl* published a long poem of mine, "The Eggboard." This poem was about my egg game and its rules. My relief *The Eggboard* (page 39) was the game's coat-of-arms, so to speak. I was particularly fascinated by time, watches, tower clocks. In the end my interpretations, my names for my plastic works, gave rise to poems. Here is a little poem in which clocks are a vital element: "A lump of masculine air disguised as an old Egyptian made himself two clocks, one from tortoises for the slow days, one from swallows for the fast days."

Suddenly my need for interpretation vanished, and the body, the form, the supremely perfected work became everything to me. In 1930 I went back to the activity which the Germans so eloquently call *Hauerei* (hewing). I engaged in sculpture and modeled in plaster. The first products were two torsos. Then came the "Concretions." Concretion signifies the natural process of condensation, hardening, coagulating, thickening, growing together. Concretion designates

Automatic Drawing. 1918. Ink, 10⅝ x 8⅜". Collection Mr. and Mrs. Morton G. Neumann, Chicago

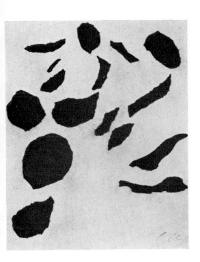

Papier Déchiré. 1932. Collage, 17⅛ x 14¾″. Collection the artist

the solidification of a mass. Concretion designates curdling, the curdling of the earth and the heavenly bodies. Concretion designates solidification, the mass of the stone, the plant, the animal, the man. Concretion is something that has grown. I wanted my work to find its humble, anonymous place in the woods, the mountains, in nature. Sophie and I now exhibited at the *Cercle et Carré* group, founded by Michel Seuphor. We were also active in founding *Abstraction-Création*. Both groups were dedicated to abstract painting and sculpture. The sessions in the cafés were endless. I attended gatherings in the most unlikely corners of Paris, where still more unlikely speeches were made in the most elegant style and accompanied by gestures which had no doubt been carried to a still higher degree of perfection by Louis XIV. The literary gatherings in the cafés weren't bad either. Eighteenth-century Satanism was still a favorite dish in certain literary circles. In other groups every speaker was expected to invoke the Hegelian dialectic at least once a minute. Since it was no longer possible to send *lettres de cachet* meting out sentences of exile and imprisonment, the groups had to content themselves with letters of sadistic vilification. But I never had the pleasure of hearing Breton, Eluard, or Péret read their wonderful poems.

The search for an unattainable perfection, the delusion that a work could be completely finished, became a torment. I cut the papers for my *collages* with extreme precision and smoothed them down with a special sandpaper. The slightest loose thread or fiber was intolerable to me. The tiniest crack in a bit of paper often led me to destroy a whole *collage*. This frenzy ended in a tragedy when I was asked to exhibit some old *collages* I had done in collaboration with Sophie Taeuber. This accident taught me the true meaning of perfection and finish. The word perfection means not only the fullness of life but also its end, its completion, its finish, and the word "accident" implies not only chance, fortuitous combination, but also what happens to us, what befalls us. We brought down the *collages* from the attic where they had been exposed for years to heat, cold, and dampness. Some of the papers had come unstuck, they were covered with spots, mould, and cracks, and between paper and cardboard blisters had formed that looked more loathsome to me than the bloated bellies of drowned rats. When after many weeks of confusion I had calmed down a bit, I began to tear my papers instead of cutting them neatly with scissors. I tore up drawings and carelessly smeared paste over and under them. If the ink dissolved and ran, I was delighted. I stuck my *collages* together with a wad of newsprint instead of pressing them carefully with blotting paper, and if cracks developed, so much the better; as far as I was concerned, it made my work more authentic. I had accepted the transience, the dribbling away, the brevity, the impermanence, the fading, the withering, the spookishness of our existence. Not only had I accepted it, I had even welcomed transience into my work as it was coming into being. These torn pictures, these *papiers déchirés* brought me closer to a faith in things other than earthly. I exhibited them for the first time in 1933 in Jeanne Bucher's gallery in Paris, and most of them found their way to the United States. I believe that they represent the transition from abstract painting to "liberated painting," as I should like to call the new American painting. The divine dream is a bridge between too much and too little. This dream is a fundamental part of my plastic search; similarly Sophie Taeuber created her luminous dream between coming-into-being and passing-away.

In 1941 Sophie and I fled from Paris to Grasse, whence we planned to leave for the United States. In Grasse we joined our friends Sonia Delaunay, Alberto and Susi Magnelli. For two years we lived in that wonderful place, surrounded by trembling crowns of light, gliding flower wings, ringing clouds, and tried to forget the horror of the world. We did drawings, watercolors, and lithographs together, and so produced one of the most beautiful of books.[1] Every possibility of work in common was tried out in this book. Its title consists of our four names. Originally we planned to put it out anonymously. Despite the horrors of those years, I look back on this period of work with my friends as one of the finest experiences of my life. Never was there a trace of vanity, arrogance, rivalry.

When Christopher Columbus, my pet, tried to sail to the East Indies "the other way round," he discovered America. When we tried to paint "the other way round," we discovered modern painting. It now seems incredible to me that I should have taken so long to realize that the art of our century and that of the preceding centuries are entirely different things. The beauty of Rembrandt's engravings, Giotto's frescoes, or the statuary of the Gothic cathedrals has little relation to that of the painting and sculpture of our day. They are as different from one another as the beauty of the nightingale's song and the beauty of the Gregorian chant. Even more so, in fact. They are incommensurable, like the beauty of the murmuring spring and the beauty of the rose, the beauty of a poem composed by the trees and the beauty of a snowflake.

JEAN HANS ARP

Meudon, May 1958

---

[1] [J. Arp — S. Delaunay — A. Magnelli — S. Taeuber-Arp. *Les Nourritures Terrestres.* Paris, 1950.]

ARP AND THE DADA MOVEMENT

The Navel Bottle. c. 1918. Lithograph, 16⅝ x 9⅝". The Museum of Modern Art, New York, gift of J. B. Neumann

I met Arp for the first time in the Cabaret Voltaire, the famous cradle of Dadaism. The Cabaret Voltaire, located in a little restaurant in the Spiegelgasse in Zurich, had been founded by Ball, Tzara, the brothers Janco, and Arp a few weeks before I arrived. It was in February during the big war, A.D. 1916, at a time when Germany's star was already in decline and when many German prisoners of war, sent to Switzerland by the Red Cross, were to be seen in the streets.

"This is Arp," said Hugo Ball. Ball was a writer whom I had known well in Germany and with whom I had been producing lectures and publishing little unnoticed magazines. I shook hands with Arp. I had no way of knowing then that this was the beginning of a friendship with one of the greatest sculptors of our time. As a matter of fact, I did not even know that Arp was a sculptor, and later when I asked Ball what Arp did, he said: "I believe he paints."

A certain anonymity remained characteristic of Arp during all the time I was active in the Cabaret Voltaire. Arp was, I felt, a shy and withdrawn personality, utterly sensitive, but jovial and ready for a good laugh. At first I did not pay much attention to him because I was wrapped up in our work at the Cabaret. Every evening on a primitive stage Ball, Emmy Hennings, and I were desperately trying to entertain the audience by dancing, reciting poems and giving all sorts of harangues designed to stir the bourgeois out of their conventional contentment. Arp seldom if ever participated in these anti-bourgeois activities. He was always deeply involved with himself and his art. In one of his books Ball reports conversations he had with Arp at this period: "He is dissatisfied with the fat texture of the expressionist paintings. He insists on lines, structure, and a new sincerity." Arp's sincerity was very obvious. What he wanted was not the noise of the Dada movement. His interest in publicity was small. He only cared about the revolutionary implications of our artistic activities and hence of art in general.

Arp did not cease to be detached from the Cabaret after the word Dada itself came before the public and brought the founders of the Cabaret Voltaire into the spotlight in Zurich and elsewhere. All of us felt the impact of our new publicity, and we often discussed the prospects of fame. Arp alone did not seem to be very interested in all this; he lived apart and only seldom appeared at the Cabaret. At this time, Arp was already acquainted with Sophie Taeuber, who was working as an art teacher at one of the Zurich colleges. Arp introduced us to her, but Sophie also shied away from the noisy Cabaret, filled with drunken students and intellectuals, not unwilling to express their antagonism in an occasional fist fight. While Janco contributed posters for the walls of the Cabaret and made masks we esteemed highly, Arp played the role of the counselor. He talked to us about abstract art, about the Futurists, Picasso, Braque, and the cubist movement. Through him we learned about Picabia.

I enjoyed strolling with Arp often along the shores of the famous Zurich lake where the swans once had been envied by Ball and Hennings because they had regular meals. The lake was the natural meeting place for all of us, and many of our plans were discussed beside it. I remember walking with Arp one afternoon as he was telling me about his plans. He said he wanted to produce something entirely new, a form of abstraction expressing our time and our feelings about it. This "time," the impact of which we saw and felt daily in the war headlines of the newspapers, asked for, said Arp, a complete revision of all our notions about colors and forms. He talked to me about the *Blaue Reiter* group he had belonged to, about Kandinsky, Chagall, Marc, and others, only dimly known to us. When we walked together Arp was always impeccably clad. Although his great feeling for elegance and female beauty made him observe people carefully, thoughts about his work never left him. One day he asked me whether I would like to go with him to his studio and see his pictures. I went. We entered the small apartment, and I was amazed at all the objects standing around and stacked up against the walls. There were dozens of canvases, cardboards, and unfinished works of sculpture. Since the first sight was rather confusing, I stood there and didn't say anything. "This is just the beginning," said Arp. "But look at this. It will probably help you to understand what I am after . . ."

In the center of the room was an easel and on the easel a canvas of medium size on which was painted a still life of potatoes. At this time in his career Arp was still doing occasional representational pictures.

"They are ghostlike and anemic," I said.

"This is just what I am after," said Arp.

A few weeks later Arp made some severe woodcuts for my *Phantastische Gebete,* which was published in the series called Dada Collection. After this he made a few semi-abstract illustrations for another book of mine entitled *Schalaben, Schalabai, Schalamezzomai.* Our friendship became closer, and I now understood why he didn't want to participate very much in our activities at the Cabaret. He was still struggling violently to make up his mind what direction his work was to take.

In Zurich things often happened which have important implications for us still today. One day Arp and I were talking about the law of chance and the problem of simultaneity, and Arp was experimenting with pieces of paper, letting them fall to the ground and then pasting them together in the order they had chosen themselves. Another day we discussed the problem of cooperation among artists as the great need of our time. He said that the artist had to find means and ways of emerging from the isolation imposed on him by our era of anti-intellectualism. The topic of cooperation as an experience was always present while we worked to-

18

gether in the Dada group, and not only then but also later Arp was intensely interested in it. He related it to the idea of complete objectivity, *la realité nouvelle*, a notion the full impact of which came out years after.

This was the miracle of Dada, that it gave all of us the courage to say what seemed to be so impossible to convey to anybody, and this courage benefited Arp more than any of us, as he was shy and detached by nature. "It was," he once said to me "like having waited for a long time in the dark and then having been aroused by a loud signal. I stepped forward, and I thought there would be nothing but catcalls. But there were all of you, friends, interested and full of praise."

In a way Dada was for Arp a sort of clarifying and intensifying possibility. Here in Zurich with all his friends around, he was able to bring into pictorial and sculptural reality what he had been thinking for a long time. Arp was always and, of course, especially at this time full of the essential Dada spirit, the irony, and the critical attitude, not only toward art but also toward the world as such and the world within ourselves. "The Dadaist," as Hugo Ball has said, "is a man who laughs about himself."

Though this existential and paradoxical attitude appeared in many of his remarks, letters and poems, Arp never lost his basic seriousness. He tended in general toward a certain severity. Even when he was associated with Schwitters, years after, he seldom worked with the shock technique of what we used to call the new material — match boxes, egg shells, hair of dolls and dogs pasted directly into the painting. Arp's personal nobility, his classical, pure approach to art as well as life, made it difficult for him to produce that bit of vulgarity we see so often in Dada works.

There is another characteristic of Arp, which should not be forgotten — his playfulness and a certain childlike joy, his wistful understanding of embarrassing situations. Once after he had been a guest at one of the luxury hotels in St. Moritz he told me, laughing, about something which had impressed him deeply. He had seen American women dancing without shoes. "Think of this," he said, "they get rid of their shoes and dance." "Why?" I asked. "It's very simple," he said, "because they dance better without."

The playfulness is easily seen in Arp's work and in his constant experimentation. He was always willing to give a new idea a chance, in art and in life. But underneath, Arp has always possessed, more than anybody I know, a tremendous singleness of purpose: he never plays and forgets himself playing. Under the charming outside is always a great intensity moving toward a goal. He knows the limits of fun, and he does not hesitate to say so when he thinks the hour has struck. This unusual ability to transcend himself constantly without going astray made it possible for him to participate in a whole series of art movements without really identifying himself with anybody or anything but Arp.

RICHARD HUELSENBECK

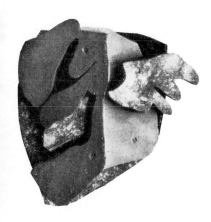

Portrait of Tzara. 1916. Painted wood relief, 18⅞ x 18¼". Collection the artist

ARP: AN APPRECIATION

Arp achieved, within a limited range of formal devices, an astonishing invention and complexity of expression. He has been creatively active not only in a variety of visual mediums, but in the art of poetry as well. From the basic energies of visual form and the word, from a continuing and fresh exploration of the relationships of planes in space, of volume, and of sounds, Arp has constructed a language of art which is expressed through symbols rather than in descriptive statements.

Early in his life, Arp indicated a desire to paint and draw. He received his first academic training under Ludwig von Hofmann in Weimar (1905–7) and at the Académie Julian in Paris (1908). By this time, he had already begun to experiment with the use of clay and to mould elementary plastic forms. During 1908 and 1909, in the Swiss town of Weggis, Arp made a group of curious paintings in which his impressions of the landscape underwent a strange transformation. Even at this time, it was not the intimate detail of natural forms that fascinated him, but their underlying organic structure, their varied rhythms, and the tensions between plane and line. To these qualities, he gave new intensity and direct expression.

One might ask which contemporary trends in art influenced him. Arp himself has noted that during his first stay in Paris, he was strongly impressed by two quite different worlds of form. On one hand, he was moved by Rouault's use of bold distortions and thick black outlines. Then too, he was impressed by the delicate, atmospheric manner in which Seurat unified the human body, particularly in his drawings, so that it took on a doll-like, magical quality. Not color but line, the silhouette, the simplified human body and its organic shape were the elements of which Arp made most striking use in his later graphic art, his reliefs, and sculpture in the round. In the 1912 number of the *Blaue Reiter* appeared some of Arp's female heads and busts and humorous vignettes emphatically outlined in black. And in the 1913 issues of *Der Sturm* were a group of his heads, figures and rhythmically accented drawings. These are the only examples which have survived from Arp's pre-Dada period, since he later was impelled to destroy all the remnants of an outgrown phase. Only from the artist, or from his friends, can one learn something about this early period of his development.

Actually it is only with the beginning of the Dada period in Zurich, from 1916 to 1919, that Arp's work takes on a distinctly personal note. He then began to work in relief and also considerably extended the scope of his experiments in graphics. The prevailing tendencies of the time in relief sculpture ranged from the classicizing of the German Adolf von Hildebrand, to the blend of antique and *Art Nouveau* in Maillol and Bourdelle, and the flamboyant Baroque of Rodin. It is apparent that Arp's elementary language of form depended upon none of these sources. Even the bold reliefs by R. Duchamp-Villon, of 1913, with their rhythmic principle of organization, can be related back to the figure compositions of traditional art. So can the architectural schemes of Archipenko's reliefs of 1915 to 1918, built up of anatomical fragments. There is, however, a historical if not a direct formal relationship between Picasso's post-1913 relief constructions — architectural ensembles of segmented forms, transposed from the medium of *collage* — and Arp's first Dada reliefs. In the latter, too, in works like the *Forest* of 1916 (page 35) and *Plant Hammer* of 1917 (page 36), one finds clusters of brightly colored, overlapping organic forms. The entirely original elements, however, are Arp's personal language of symbols, their novel form, the loosening of his composition, and his exploitation of empty space as a positive agent of visual expression. In these works, leafy undulations and rudimentary anatomical fragments appear in unusual, strongly silhouetted shapes; or the forms are condensed into vase-like shapes recalling primitive archetypes of the human figure. Simple circles and ovals also appear. A quality of dynamic life is imparted to the groups of related shapes by variations in size and scale. The emphasis on empty background areas throws into sharp relief and lends new proportions to the contrasting forms. Within the "boundlessness" of the plane surface (which seems to exist as an aspect of infinity), every formal event is enhanced, its dimensions sharpened, to become, for the eye, a new and universal alphabet of basic shapes.

Arp's symbolic language appears to express the principles of growth and continuous transformation that one finds in nature. Thus, he gives shape to the dreams of mankind. It is as if nature herself, and the circumstantial facts of physical existence, had formulated their own language of expression in the profound depths of consciousness. At the same time, all the types of form created by Arp are entirely independent of forms literally existing in nature; and they have been freed from limiting, specific detail. Particular form has become universal form, moving according to invisible forces within the cosmic scheme. Boldly, Arp fashions his image of the world in fragmentary symbols, enabling man to speak through nature, and nature through man. "Arp's hypnotic language takes us back to a lost paradise, to cosmic secrets, and teaches us to understand the language of the universe,"[2] wrote Max Ernst, in comment upon the profound romanticism of his colleague's esthetic.

Arp is not only, however, interested in the suggestive and imaginative ramifications of his symbolic forms. But he also concerns himself with their

[2] Art of this Century, New York. Exhibition of J. Arp, Feb., 1944. Preface by Max Ernst.

grouping, and with their contrapuntal and harmonic interplay, frequently calling them "constellations." He evolves structures of a fluid order, in which the elements are disposed according to "the laws of chance." These structures are outgrowths of Arp's acceptance of freedom, the freedom of unconscious forces, not, as is so often wrongly assumed,[3] of chaos. In these reliefs, forms speak simply and sensitively to one another across their spatial planes. They speak in a dialogue which calls to mind the clownish mutterings of James Joyce's Jute and Mute,[4] and primeval rock formations. The dialogue is carried on in our modern idiom, but it constantly renews itself from these primal sources. Thus, the image of the world revealed with such austerity by Arp, is constructed of profound and buried memories, and reflects a philosophy blended out of humor and wisdom. Arp again and again protests with deliberate simplicity against the alienating rationalism which has thrust man into his singularly exposed position. Humbly, he tries to restore man to his place in the natural order. Nature's cycle of growth and change, of becoming and dissolution, constitute the universal theme of his art. He is not interested in the abundance and manifold fertility of nature. What he wishes to express in visual form is the law unifying all natural processes. And he sets out to show that the same law orders the fundamental process of artistic creation.

In works like the wood relief *Bird Mask* of 1918 (opposite), simple and yet complex forms are given expression in Arp's language of fantasy. Here the structure — perforations and silhouette — somewhat resemble the branch of a tree, an egg, a beak, and an eye, all addressing us in unison. Sometimes Arp fuses his shapes by means of his unifying modulations. He also produces works which are more loosely organized, in which commonplace objects like forks, flasks, anchors, neckties, boots, and so forth, are animated by being set into a kind of alliance with organic shapes and anatomical fragments. All these objects are thus endowed with mutual vitality, by being induced into combination with others upon the universal picture plane.

Arp uses wood, cardboard and even string — a medium of expression with stirring calligraphic connotations originated by this artist. Their very titles, such as *Objects Ordered in a Calligraphic Manner*, of 1928, give voice to this quality.

More and more in the reliefs of his later years, Arp discarded the mocking methods by which he had once interrogated the disordered world while, at the same time, giving them through his imagery a fresh compositional unity. Gradually after 1929, he abandoned those earlier, Dada-like forms which were launched to shock, and began to emphasize, with a new spirit of detachment, the world of organic growth and structure which encompasses our lives. Here one finds those "neutral forms against an indefinable neutral background," as Mondrian

[3] B. Sedlmayr, *Die Revolution der modernen Kunst.* Hamburg: Rowohlt-Verlag, 1955.
[4] James Joyce, *Finnegans Wake.* New York: Viking Press, 1939.

Bird Mask. 1918. Wood.
Formerly Doucet Foundation, Paris.
(Not exhibited)

admiringly described them.[5] Arp's chief concern in these works was to bring elements of geometric as well as of organic structure into equilibrium. Ovals and rotating forms, periods, commas, or rudimentary shapes with undulating, organic surfaces are distributed, balanced and grouped into constellations upon a plane. Some works are tentative, like *Summer Metope* of 1946 (page 81); some, like *Vegetal Symmetry* (page 80), also of 1946, are fully achieved and integrated symmetrical arrangements. Arp's struggle to achieve an absolute compositional balance in these reliefs reminds one of certain graphic work of his Dada period, such as the illustrations for R. Huelsenbeck's *Phantastische Gebete* of 1916, or for T. Tzara's *De Nos Oiseaux* of 1923.

After 1941, Arp used marble and bronze in addition to his earlier materials. Stone inspired him to an architectonic severity. In linear compositions of an amazing incisiveness such as *Structure of White Blossoms for My Dead Wife* of 1943 (page 79) and *Mediterranean Sculpture II* of 1941 — fantastic planes emerge,

[5] P. Mondrian, "New Art — New Life." In H. L. C. Jaffé *De Stijl 1917–31.* Amsterdam: Meulenhoff, 1956. (p. 211–254)

and forms are dispersed in an animated interplay between inner and outer spheres, while still retaining organic vibrations. In his metal works, on the other hand, serpentine plant rhythms are brought into play. Now, along with his curving symbolic images, Arp articulates also strict architectonic constructions in planes, using these both in succession and simultaneously. And, ever since the Dada period, even in his graphic work, Arp succeeds in expressing a paradoxical combination of mocking fantasy and classical serenity. By 1916, Arp had begun to illustrate the covers and pages of Dada publications (*Dada* numbers 1–6, 1916 and 1917; *Zeltweg* of 1919), accompanying his own poetry and that of his friends. To these pages he gave a quality of monumentality by his expressive use of rhythmic black and white areas. Here, as before, one is struck by the imaginative freedom with which Arp orchestrates an individual form or groups of forms. One is impressed by the originality of image and by the way in which Arp combines type and the blank areas of the page. His method led the way to radically new departures in book design and advertising art: the eye takes note of the basic forms, while at the same time, one has a sense of fluid lines of movement and an austere composition. This is a totally new kind of book "illumination," as opposed to "illustration," even when one compares them to the early woodcuts of Kandinsky, introduced in his book *The Art of Spiritual Harmony* of 1912, and particularly in his collection of poems *Klänge*, 1913. Arp's "organic constructions," as he came to call them, convey an impression of greater lyricism. Kandinsky's flaming expressions, on the other hand, seem to spring from a very different, entirely dramatic, impulse. Even in these graphic works, Arp was concerned with the "structure of vegetal matter," as he called it. At one and the same time, he used combinations of organic and geometric shapes. Employed together, these two varieties of image produce an ambiguous effect, which enhanced the remarkable double-level of his art at that time. Actually, these two methods later diverged to become the two decisive directions of expression of our time.

Perhaps it is surprising to note that Arp developed the severe — one might almost call it the classical — *collage*, in 1916, in the very midst of the revolutionary Dada period. The previous two years had seen more turbulent experiments in the use of contrasting materials. But in Arp's few works of that period (some in collaboration with Sophie Taeuber) which still exist, one sees a rectangular space organized into balanced proportions, accented with colors of extreme finesse. These geometrical *collages* are built of silver-grey, black, white, and ochre paper cuttings. They tell us a great deal about the particular mental climate in which Arp created them: the other side of the Dada world, in which the focus was not only upon a condition of wild upheaval, but also upon a mystical world-view. Another artist who tried to encourage this philosophical attitude was Hugo Ball, author, performer, and head of the Zurich Cabaret Voltaire. Both he and Arp stood out against a wave of materialism and the threat which mechanization

Automatic Drawing. 1916. Ink, 16¾ x 21¼".
The Museum of Modern Art, New York

then seemed to pose, of turning men into robots. They held that only the admission of a "mystical reality," as Arp liked to call it, could help man to build up his defenses against the dangers of his own time. And to this day, Arp's viewpoint continues to be applicable in terms of universal need.

His *collages,* which were produced in a spirit of impersonality, cut out as it were anonymously, by machine, became the agents of his protest against the ingenious virtuosity of much art of the time — those clever artistic tricks which threatened to stifle the qualities of spirituality and originality which inhabit the true work of art. After all, Arp's *collages* were intended as proclamations of a new order of simplicity and devoutness, and to this end, he used the most humble means of expression. They were different from the cubist *collages,* which fused fragmented parts of reality into an abstract composition. Arp wished to construct calm images for meditation, of the same order which had its highest and most spiritual flowering in the later works of Mondrian.

Just how complex were his thought and sensitivity, and on how many levels he existed, Arp had revealed in his earliest years. It may remain a unique fact, that this art with its simple forms and its elemental structure, was able to express such a rich and variegated world of the spirit. Under Arp's hands during the course of his life, the art of *collage* underwent many transformations. After 1930, he occasionally worked in "torn-paper." This mode expressed Arp's awareness of the tragic tenor of his time, and its predominate note of destructiveness. The artist had watched his own earlier *collages,* so carefully constructed, turn yellow and torn, and fall to pieces. Now intentionally, he introduced the ravages and havoc of time into his compositions. Anticipating the process of disintegration, he tried to suggest the tragic passage of time to which all material things are victim. With this method he seemed to introduce time itself into art.

25

Arp's graphics, reliefs, and sculptures in their emphasis on animated spatial relations, were destined to play an important role in architecture. In the interior of the Strasbourg Aubette, the frescoes he created in 1927 and 1928 with Theo van Doesburg and Sophie Taeuber, were completely in the spirit of and even enhanced the atmosphere of this dance hall — in spite of their free, grotesque form and content. Huge mushroom-shaped beings, almost entirely head, and spinning navel shapes seemed to spring from a primeval realm, while their proportions and the manner in which they were spaced on the wall lent a sharp rhythmic accent and a sense of animated fantasy to the walls of the interior.

The wood reliefs for the bar of the Harvard Graduate Center, which Walter Gropius commissioned Arp to do in 1950 are more lyrical, less like scherzos than the Strasbourg frescoes which are unfortunately now destroyed. Like stars and clouds, filled with manifold meanings and ever transforming themselves, these creatures of the imagination pass across the horizontal plane. In his *Configuration,* made in 1956 for the University of Caracas, spiked metal forms float in groups before the clay wall. Somewhat like East Asian characters, these figures cast a lively shadow-play upon the background, and thus exist on a second level, in the shape of their reflection.

Arp's graphic work has, too, an often markedly monumental quality. One happens upon these lithographs and woodcuts, tacked at random to the wall of a private room or a public place like a bar or café; and instantly one sees the image take on an intense and close correspondence to the room as a whole. The composition and forms vibrate in an astonishing manner quite in unison with the architectural ambiance, almost as if they had been destined to form part of it from the very beginning.

Seen as a whole, the art of Jean Arp, with its deep humanity, has let into the world an enchanting ray of fantasy and irrationality. And it has achieved this at a moment in history when the world is being propelled by technology and bureaucracy in an ever more restricted course. Directed from within by a mysterious principle of order, his art retains its spontaneity without ever ignoring discipline or falling into chaos. His is an art which obeys the "laws of chance," but never chance itself. Within its confines, age-old memories of mankind are released from their deep dwelling-places and well up to suffuse the primitive forms. But also our modern sensibility responds to these forms, and through them, we re-explore the very springs and roots of our visual art. For Arp's goal was "Construction in terms of lines, planes, shapes, and colors . . . despising artifice, presumption, imitation, and the carnival tricks of the trade. For art should aspire to the spiritual, to a mystical reality."

CAROLA GIEDION-WELCKER

ON SOME OF ARP'S RELIEFS

Arp writes in German and French, but his best known statement — the one which begins "Art is a fruit" — made its first public appearance in English: it was published in the magazine *Transition* in 1932, in a piece called "Notes from a Dada Diary," translated from the German by Eugène Jolas. The Jolas translation reflects the spirit of the comical and beautiful objects which Arp contributed out of the goodness of his heart to Dada and Surrealism. This is the relevant passage, which was printed entirely in lower case: *art is a fruit growing out of man like the fruit out of a plant like the child out of the mother. while the fruit of the plant grows independent forms and never resembles a balloon or a president in a cutaway suit the artistic fruit of man shows for the most part a ridiculous resemblance to the appearance of other things. reason tells man to stand above nature and to be the measure of all things. thus man thinks he is able to live and to create against the laws of nature and he creates abortions. through reason man became a tragic and ugly figure. i dare say he would create even his children in the form of vases with umbilical cords if he could do so. reason has cut man off from nature.*

Arp must have written this passage entirely for his own pleasure. I do not know the date of his original manuscript, but the reference to children in the form of vases with umbilical cords is a reminder that one of his lithographs, published by Merz in 1923, is of a vase-shaped personage with a large hat and even larger belly button, which he described, with a nonsensical allusiveness worthy of Lear, as a "navel bottle." In any case, devices which he himself identifies with amphorae and navels are among those which come most persistently and naturally from his hand, and by gleefully and arbitrarily embellishing his argument with mementoes of his own kind of "artistic fruit" he managed to slip "tragic and ugly" man a brotherly handshake whilst giving him a good dressing-down.

When a revised version of the "Art is a fruit" passage appeared in *On My Way* in 1948, it had become conventionally meaningful. The syntax was on its dignity and the glee had evaporated: *Art is a fruit that grows in man, like a fruit on a plant, or a child in its mother's womb. But whereas the fruit of the plant, the fruit of the animal, the fruit in the mother's womb, assume autonomous and natural forms, art, the spiritual fruit of man, usually shows an absurd resemblance to the aspect of something else. Only in our own epoch have painting and sculpture been liberated from the aspect of a mandolin, a president in a Prince Albert, a battle, a landscape. I love nature but not its substitutes. Naturalist, illusionist art is a substitute for nature.*

This version goes better with Arp's sculpture in the round than with the reliefs that he made between 1916 and 1932. The biomorphic forms which he has carved or modeled since 1930 or thereabouts make overt allusions to vegetable and animal life; they could be the fruit that grows on not too unlikely trees and in almost possible wombs: they provide excellent illustrations of the notion that the artist is a fruit-bearing organism and they opened up a useful line of communication with the general public. Between the writing of the first and second version of this statement, Arp's attitude to the creative faculty underwent a change, of which one symptom was the dropping of the small " i " for the self. The amended version was made by a man who was shouldering the burden of an artistic reputation.

There is no sharp division between Arp's Dada and surrealist work. It is true that the beginning of the period of his active collaboration with the Surrealists (he participated in the first surrealist exhibition, held at the Galerie Pierre in 1925) coincided with a new informality in the disposition of the forms in his reliefs which was probably provoked by the most famous of surrealist texts — Lautréamont's "as beautiful as the chance meeting of an umbrella and a sewing-machine on an operating table" — but the "chance meetings" were between anonymous forms which only assumed identities after Arp had given them names. He was already constructing pictographs of the world in some of his Dada reliefs, and in his surrealist period these pictographs tended to become more simple in appearance and more economical in the use of expressive symbols.

By the same token, it is not possible to put a precise date to the end of his surrealist period. There is no break in the continuity of his work that can be linked with the year, generally put at 1928, in which he severed his connection with the surrealist group. The reliefs became even more simple and economical after that date, but the spirit in which the surrealist reliefs were conceived was never stronger than in certain examples made in 1931 and 1932. I think it can be said, however, that when he became preoccupied by sculpture in the round he began to assume that the product of the artist's creative faculty proved itself to be a natural conception if it bore a kind of family resemblance to objects formed by natural processes: he has not been rigid or fanatical about it, but it leaves a mark of sensual solemnity upon even those works which are not noticeably biomorphic, and his later reliefs, which are often very beautiful, have a certain sculptural sumptuousness which was not attained, and certainly not sought, in the reliefs made before 1932.

Arp once said: "My reliefs and sculptures fit naturally in nature." This is true of the sculpture, and I can think of no twentieth-century works which sit more snugly in a patch of grass than his "human concretions" made in 1935; but

Madame Torso with Wavy Hat. 1916. Wood, 15⅞ x 10¾".
Collection Hermann Rupf, Bern. (Not exhibited)

the painted reliefs are very far from being at home in nature. Their profoundly human qualities are inseparable from the fact that they are highly unnatural-looking objects, and if one came across one of them in a Nature Reserve it would declare that it carried a human message as boldly and intransigently as the painted notice boards that tell one how to get out again.

According to Hans Bolliger, Arp did not begin to make painted wood reliefs until 1917, but Carola Giedion-Welcker assigns the relief called *Forest* (page 35) to the previous year, and I think it must be a very early example because, unlike the other reliefs of the period, it makes formal allusions to a predetermined subject matter. The tree, the moon, and the dark forest floor were clearly in mind at the time they were shaped, and the work as a whole may well have been conceived as a concretion of the overlapping forms and shallow planes in Rousseau's jungles.

In a larger work called *Plant Hammer* (page 36), dated 1917, which was made like the *Forest,* with one piece of wood impacted upon another, the profiles follow a more arbitrary course, and it is evident from the curious and rather strained title, that Arp discovered the subject after examining the finished work. The forms are ambiguous, and I suspect that Arp was attempting through the title to exercise control over the suggestiveness of the image: by identifying the curvilinear silhouettes with plant life he was perhaps hoping to distract attention from their even stronger resemblance to reptilian life. Arp was highly conscious of the magic of words and the weight of associations they carry, and it was his preference for understatement in his titles that turned his reliefs into object-poems. If he had brought the reptilian aspect of the shapes in *Plant Hammer* into the title it would have translated the image into a somewhat banal emblem of good and evil. At all events, he seems to have put a curb on his curvilinear gestures in other Dada reliefs; the curves of *Madame Torso with Wavy Hat* (page 29) and the superbly inventive raggedness of *Bird Mask* (page 23) exemplify his ability to exercise some control over shape-making actions which remained essentially arbitrary.

There is a macabre element in *Bird Mask* which he could undoubtedly have nurtured and developed if he had wished. He was on terms of intimacy with Dadas and Surrealists who were practising various kinds of pictorial terrorism and he must have been tempted at every turn. As a northern artist, he would have been following the line of least resistance if he had allowed the scarifying image to flourish in his work, but macabre and horrific elements play only a minor and scarcely perceptible role in his reliefs.

In the early twenties, he began to devise reliefs composed of several pieces of wood cut into simple shapes and scattered over an irregular or rectangular backboard like a crazy game of checkers. Among the first were the "clock" reliefs in which the hands part company, wander across a face which has lost all its numerals, and "register" biological time by changing their shape and laying eggs. In many that followed, he adopted the convention of the enigmatic encounter, which was being used by other Surrealists for the production of brutal or fantastic relationships in the manner of Lautréamont's famous image. But even those examples which most obviously disclose Arp's use of this system, such as the painted wood *Shirt Front and Fork* (page 38) and the painted cardboard *Eye and Navel Dress* acknowledge Surrealism more in the relationship between image and title than in the relationship between the forms. The forms are too

Infinite Amphora. 1929. Painted wood, 57⅛ x 44⅞". Collection Mme Carola Giedion-Welcker, Zurich. (Not exhibited)

ambiguous and too remote from illusionism to display outré disruptions of reality: their relationships are never established by perverse interferences; on the contrary, they reflect Arp's vision of a smiling world of elementary forms where nothing is incongruous.

The shirt front in *Shirt Front and Fork* is just as distinctly a human mask, and the fork is equally suggestive of a human arm, but Arp obtains his most far-reaching effects from forms which are neutral and innocuous rather than ambiguous. These wooden blanks or counters look rather like discarded cut-outs from simple fretwork panels, and at their most complicated are shaped like bits of kindergarten jigsaw puzzles or fancy biscuits. They are never "readymades" however, and even the plain discs which he has so frequently called navels are always slightly but tellingly out of true, and as soon as he places them on one of his "carefree" grounds they become, in the language of the numinous side of existentialism, rich noughts. His sense of the validity of such forms was probably influenced by Kandinsky's ideas about the spirituality of non-figurative art, and the painted wood relief called *Infinite Amphora* (page 31) shows how brilliantly he could transform one of Kandinsky's "geometrical situations."

The *Infinite Amphora* is one of Arp's greatest and most poetic works and is achieved by almost farcically simple means. A small, roughly circular disc, painted grey, with two little bulges at opposite points of its circumference, stands for an amphora with a neck at each end; it has been stuck on to a rectangular board painted light blue; the blue ground is broken by two areas of flat white paint which appear to be issuing from the necks of the amphora; they broaden into misshapen triangles as they stream away in opposite directions. The configuration brings to mind Kandinsky's contention that "the impact of the acute angle of a triangle on a circle produces an effect no less powerful than the finger of God touching the finger of Adam in Michelangelo," but Arp does not think in catastrophic terms, and Kandinsky's vision of an overwhelmingly expressive geometry has been re-cast into a marvellous genetical image. In effect, it is a purification of Tintoretto's famous anthropomorphic image of the milky way: it emblemizes a sharper comprehension of the vastness of the universe and a more profound awareness of the mystery of creation. It is an example of what Arp himself once referred to as "games of wisdom and clairvoyance which were to cure human beings of the raging madness of genius and return them modestly to their rightful place in nature."

The *Infinite Amphora* is one of a number of works which might be described as the relief maps of a poetic cosmogony: they appear to relate to Arp's avowed interest in the Pre-Socratic philosophers, and in particular to their speculations upon the originative material of things and the coherence of the natural world.

The ease with which the elementary forms in the reliefs called *Flight of*

Birds and *Constellation of Leaves* refer to larger and vaguer entities than those he names, can be partially accounted for by his response to some of the cosmogonical conceptions of the Pre-Socratics. It does not seem to me to be incongruous to relate Arp's simple counters to those "whole-natured forms" which, in the cosmogony of Empedocles, had no distinction of parts and represented a stage in both the cosmic cycle and the evolution of living things; and if we permit ourselves to see Arp's counters as the first issue of the originative substance, the board on which he raises them becomes the originative substance itself — the primeval waters of Thales, or the Indefinite of Anaximander, or the void of the Pythagoreans, which had the function of keeping things apart.

Arp usually refers to the simplest of his forms as navels, but they are also "other worlds," and this range of allusiveness is a reminder that Pre-Socratic speculations upon the origins of the universe were colored by analogies with genetics.

His extraordinary ability to scatter forms over a surface "according to the laws of chance" and turn the unexpected into the inevitable is intuitive, unique, and unassailable: nevertheless, he takes a philosophical view of chance, and indicates clearly enough in the following quotation from *On My Way* that he thinks of it as something immensely superior to the merely accidental: *The law of chance, which embraces all laws and is unfathomable like the first cause from which all life arises, can only be experienced through complete devotion to the unconscious.* He is thus able to treat the activity which brings about his "constellations" of forms as a very small and very large event. It is a gambler's throw that obeys the same law which, in the atomic theories of Leucippus and Democritus, causes the intervals between the "innumerable worlds" to be unequal. Arp's sense of placing creates a great stirring and rustling among the forms, as if they were leaves in a summer gale and as if they were stars blown into random clusters by cosmic winds. He is a humorous and undemonstrative deviser of vast conceptions.

We admire in others the evidence of tensions and anxieties and heroic labors that have sustained their venturesomeness, but in Arp we admire a venturesomeness that has involved a surrender to simple states of goodness and happiness and raised his work to the plane of leisure.

Robert Melville

Static Composition. 1915. Oil on cardboard, 35⅜ x 30¼". Collection François Arp, Paris

Left: *Rectangles Arranged According to the Laws of Chance*. 1916. Collage, 9⅞ x 4⅞". Collection the artist

Below: *Forest*. 1916. Painted wood relief, 12⅞ x 7½". Collection Roland Penrose, London

Plant Hammer. 1917. Painted wood relief, 24¾ x 19⅝″. Collection the artist

Squares Arranged According to the Laws of Chance. 1916–17. Collage, 19⅛ x 13⅝″. The Museum of Modern Art, New York. Purchase

Duo-Collage. 1918. (Executed in collaboration with Sophie Taeuber-Arp.) Paper on cardboard, 33⅞ x 26″. Collection Mr. and Mrs. Burton G. Tremaine, Meriden, Conn.

Above: *Shirt Front and Fork.* 1922. Painted wood, 22 x 27½″. Collection Mr. and Mrs. George Heard Hamilton, New Haven, Conn.

Right: *Birds in an Aquarium.* c. 1920. Painted wood, 9⅞ x 8″. The Museum of Modern Art, New York. Purchase

Egg Board. 1922. Painted wood, 29½ x 39″. Collection Fernand C. Graindorge, Liège, Belgium

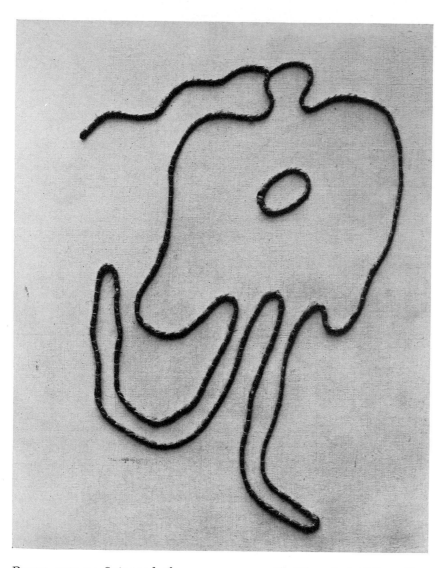

Dancer. 1923–24. String and oil on canvas, 20 x 15¾″. Sidney Janis Gallery, New York

Plate, Fork, and Navel. 1923. Painted wood relief, 23¼ x 24″. Sidney Janis Gallery, New York

Moon Frog. 1924. Oil on cardboard with cut-outs, 20½ x 27½″. Collection Mme Marguerite Hagenbach, Basel

Mountain, Table, Anchors, Navel. 1925. Oil on cardboard with cut-outs, 29⅜ x 23½". The Museum of Modern Art, New York. Purchase

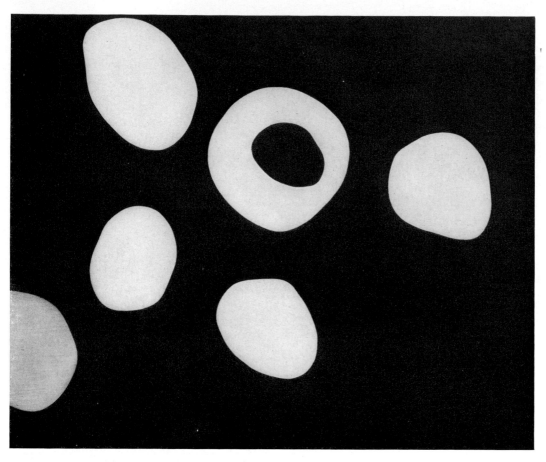

Navels. 1926. Oil on canvas, 19¾ x 23⅝". Collection Mme Marguerite Hagenbach, Basel

Abstract Composition. 1926. Oil on canvas, 22¾ x 26″. Collection Mr. and Mrs. G. David Thompson, Pittsburgh

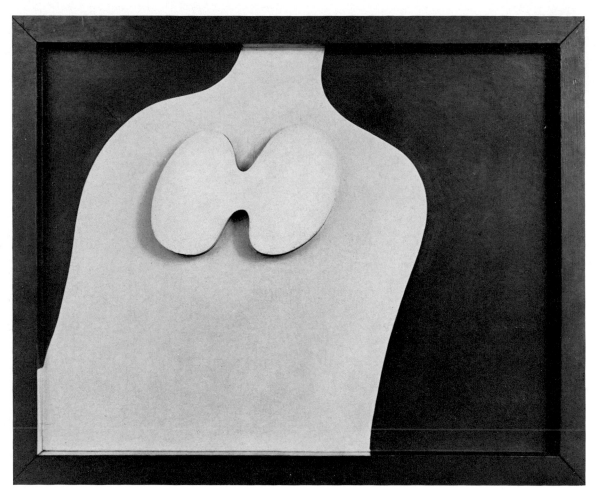

Shirt and Tie. 1928. Painted wood relief, 31⅜ x 39⅜″. Private collection, New York

Arranged According to the Laws of Chance. 1929. Painted wood relief, 55⅛ x 42⅛″. Private collection, Switzerland

Leaf. 1929. Oil and string on canvas, 28¾ x 23½″. Private collection, New York

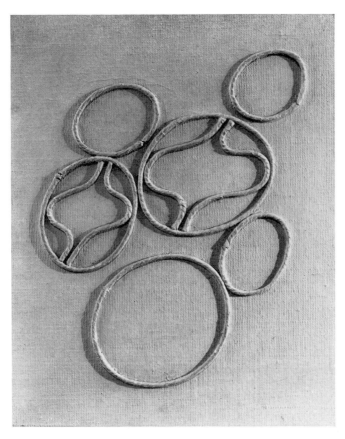

Leaves and Navels. 1929. Oil and string on canvas, 13¾ x 10¾". The Museum of Modern Art, New York. Purchase

Right: *Objects Arranged According to the Laws of Chance or Navels.* 1930. Varnished wood relief, 10⅝ x 11⅛". The Museum of Modern Art, New York. Purchase

Torso, Navel, Head with Moustache. 1930. Painted wood relief, 31½ x 39¼″. Collection Mrs. Albert H. Newman, Chicago

Two Heads. 1929. Painted wood relief, 47¼ x 39¼". The Museum of Modern Art, New York. Purchase

Hand Fruit. 1930. Painted wood, 21⅝ x 34⅝″. Private collection, Switzerland

Right: *To be Lost in the Woods.* 1932. Bronze sculpture in three forms: large, 8¾″ long; medium 4¾″ long; small 3⅜″ long. Base: 24″ high. Collection Sidney Janis, New York

Below: *Bell and Navels.* 1931. Painted wood, 10¼ x 19¼″. Collection the artist

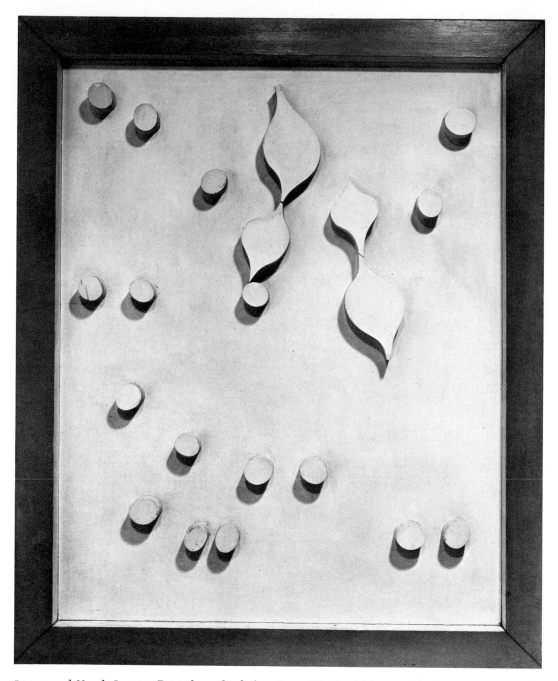

Leaves and Navels I. 1930. Painted wood relief, 31¾ x 39¾″. The Museum of Modern Art, New York. Purchase

Configuration. 1930. Painted wood relief, 27½ x 33½″. Philadelphia Museum of Art, A. E. Gallatin Collection

Arrow Cloud. 1932. Painted wood relief, 43¼ x 55⅛″. Private collection, Basel

Variation I — Constellation with Five White and Two Black Forms. 1932. Painted wood relief, 23½ x 29½".
Munson-Williams-Proctor Institute, Utica, New York

Torn Drawing. 1932. Collage, 20⅞ x 18⅛″. Collection the artist

Navel and Winged Navel. 1933. Collage, 15¾ x 13½″. Collection François Arp, Paris

Construction. 1934. Oil on board with cut-outs, 28½ x 40". Collection Mr. and Mrs. Herbert M. Rothschild, Kitchawan, New York

Metamorphosis (Shell-Swan-Swing). 1935. Bronze, 27⅛″ high. Collection the artist

Human Concretion on Oval Bowl. 1935. Bronze. Sculpture, 18¼″ high; bowl, 28⅜″ long. Collection the artist

Marital Sculpture. 1937. Wood (lathe-turned and sawed, executed in collaboration with Sophie Taeuber-Arp), 15⅜″ high. Collection the artist

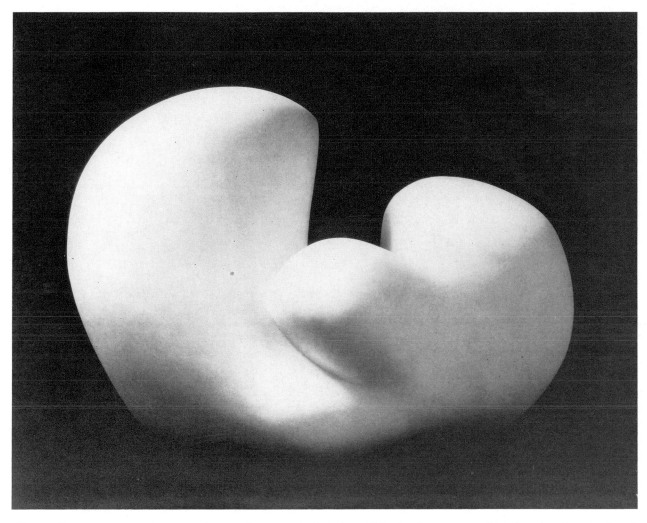

Human Concretion. 1935. Cast stone (1949, after original plaster), 19½″ high. The Museum of Modern Art, New York, gift of the Advisory Committee

Above: *Composition*. 1937. Torn paper, with India ink wash, 11½ x 12¾″. Philadelphia Museum of Art, A. E. Gallatin Collection

Right: *Composition*. 1937. Torn paper, with India ink wash and pencil, 11¾ x 9″. Philadelphia Museum of Art, A. E. Gallatin Collection

Opposite page: Rug. 1938. Wool, 78 x 59½″. The Museum of Modern Art, New York. Purchase

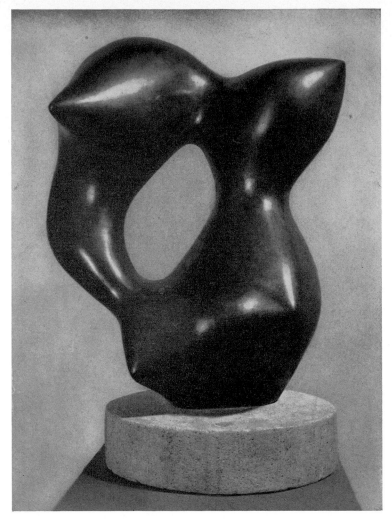

Crown of Buds. 1936. Bronze (1947, after original limestone), 18½" high. Collection Mr. and Mrs. Samuel M. Kootz, New York

Automatic Sculpture (Homage to Rodin). 1938. Granite, 10¼" high. Collection Mr. and Mrs. Richard K. Weil, St. Louis

Growth. 1938. Bronze, 31½″ high. Philadelphia Museum of Art

Lunar Armor. 1938. Granite, 15″ high. Collection Mr. and Mrs. Harry L. Winston, Birmingham, Michigan

Pre-Adamic Torso. 1938. Limestone, 18⅞″ high. Collection Mme Marguerite Hagenbach, Basel

Stone Formed by the Human Hand. 1938. Jura limestone, 16¼″ high. Kunstmuseum, Basel, Emanuel Hoffmann Fund

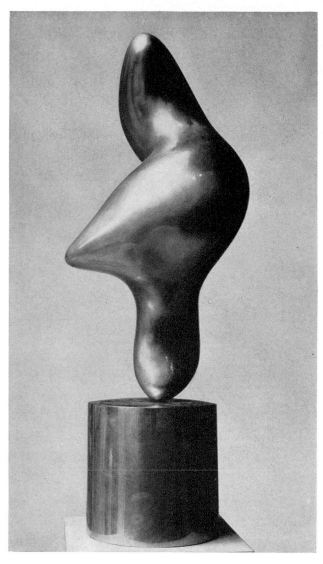

Awakening. 1938. Bronze (1958, after original plaster), 18⅝″ high. Collection Mr. and Mrs. Joseph Slifka, New York

Pre-Adamic Fruit. 1938. Bronze, 11¼″ high. Museum of Art, University of Michigan, Ann Arbor

Leaf of the Pyramids. 1939. Granite, 18″ long. The Baltimore Museum of Art, Charles and Elsa Hutzler Memorial Collection

Shell Crystal. 1938. Granite, 13″ high. Collection Nelson A. Rockefeller, New York

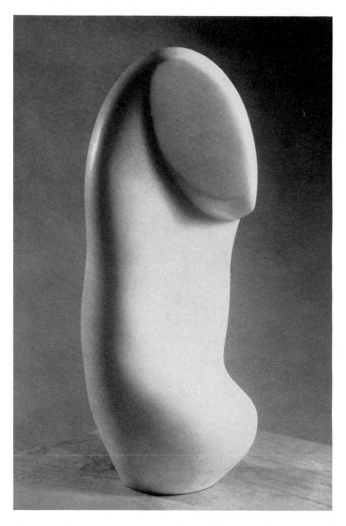

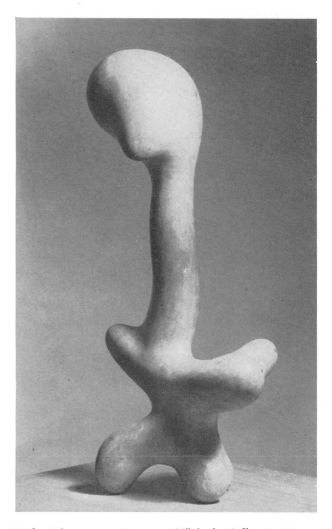

Concrete Sculpture. 1942. Marble, 14⅛" high. Collection Miss Pamela T. Colin, New York, courtesy Mr. and Mrs. Ralph F. Colin

Little Sphinx. 1942. Bronze, 16⅛" high. Collection Mr. and Mrs. Joseph Slifka, New York

Dream Amphora. 1941. Marble, 9″ high. Collection Mr. and Mrs. Herbert Bayer, Aspen, Colorado

Snake Bread. 1942. Granite, 10¼″ long. Collection Mr. and Mrs. Frederick Zimmermann, New York

Three Constellations of Same Forms. 1942.
Left to right: Numbers 1, 2, 3.
Painted wood reliefs, 35¾ x 28″ each.
Private collection, Basel

Birdlike Cloud. 1943. Painted wood relief, 32½ x 28″. Collection Dr. and Mrs. Charles R. Hulbeck, New York

Structure of White Blossoms for My Dead Wife. 1943. Painted wood relief, 55⅛ x 43¾″. Collection Mme Marguerite Hagenbach, Basel

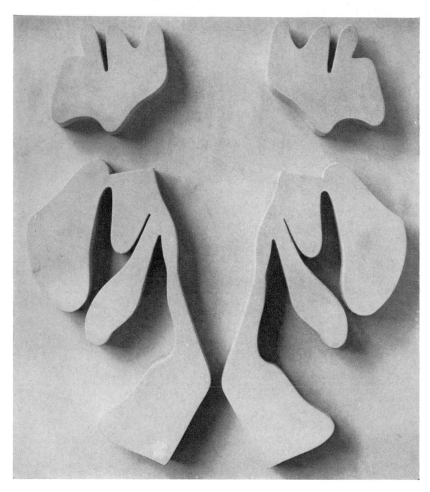

Vegetal Symmetry. 1946. Wood relief, 21⅝ x 19¼". Collection Mme Carola
Giedion-Welcker, Zurich

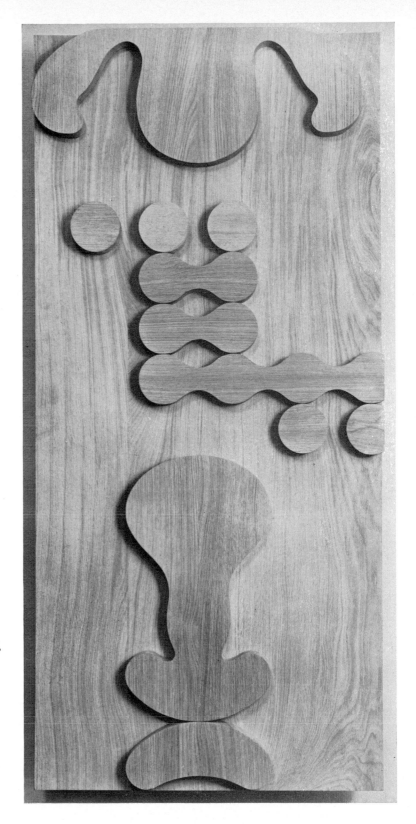

Summer Metope. 1946. Wood relief,
55⅞″ x 25⅝″. Collection the artist

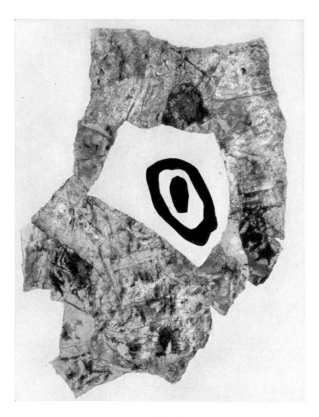

Drawing and Torn and Colored Papers. 1946. Collage, 13¾ x 9⅞". Collection Mr. and Mrs. Wackernagel-Hagenbach, Basel

Torn Drawing with Watercolor. 1946. Collage, 13¾ x 9¾". Collection Mme Marguerite Hagenbach, Basel

82

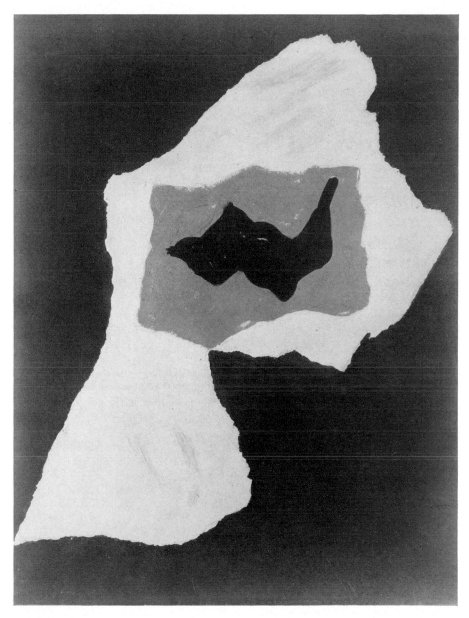

Color Tear. 1947. Collage and gouache, 24¾ x 19″. Collection Mr. and Mrs. William Jaffe, New York

Tree of Bowls. 1947. Bronze, 39⅜" high. Collection Mr. and Mrs. Richard K. Weil, St. Louis

Chimerical Font. 1947. Bronze, 31½″ high. Collection Mr. and Mrs. George Henry Warren, New York

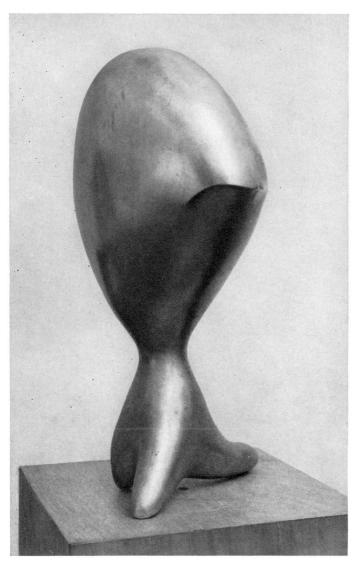

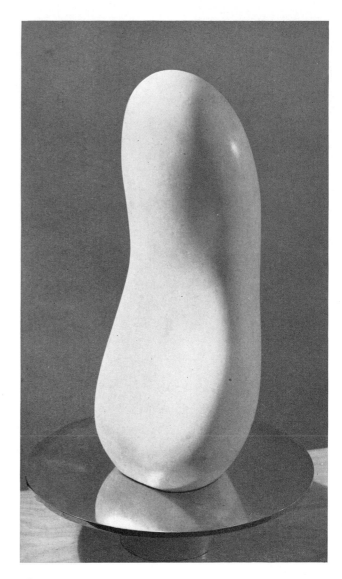

Head with Claws. 1949. Bronze, 18½″ high. Collection Joseph H. Hirshhorn, New York

Silent. 1949. Marble, 20″ high. Collection Dr. and Mrs. Israel Rosen, Baltimore

86

Owl's Dream. 1947. Marble, 15¾″ high. Collection Lee A. Ault, New York

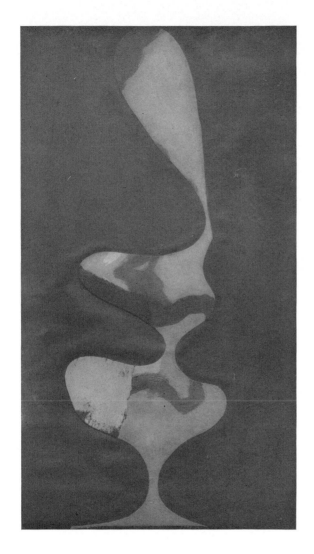

Personage. 1948. Collage and gouache,
19¼ x 10⅞″. Wellesley College
Art Museum, gift of Edgar Kaufmann

Opposite: *Pistil.* 1950. Limestone, 34⅝″ high. Collection Mr. and Mrs. Morton D. May, St. Louis

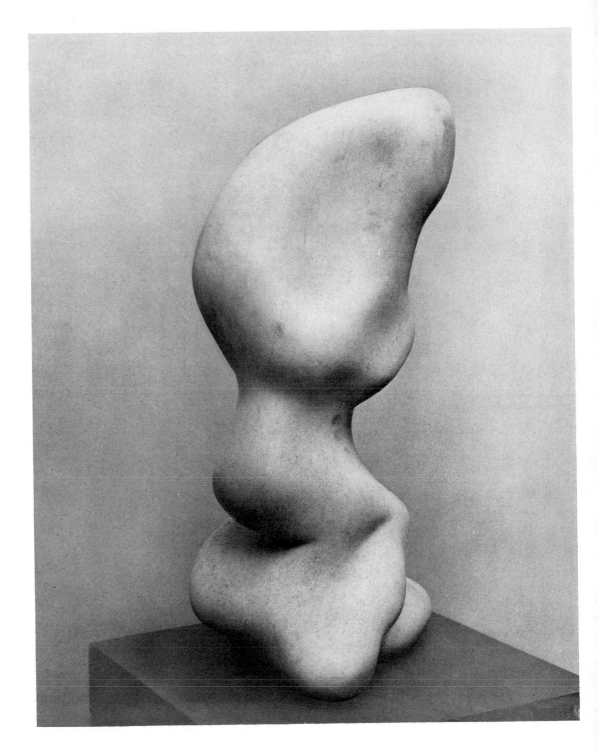

89

Above: *Star Seed*. 1949. Painted wood, 17½ x 24½". Collection Mrs. Maurice E. Culberg, Chicago

Right: *In the Manner of Papiers Déchirés*. 1949. Collage, 14¾ x 12⅞". Collection Dr. and Mrs. Charles R. Hulbeck, New York

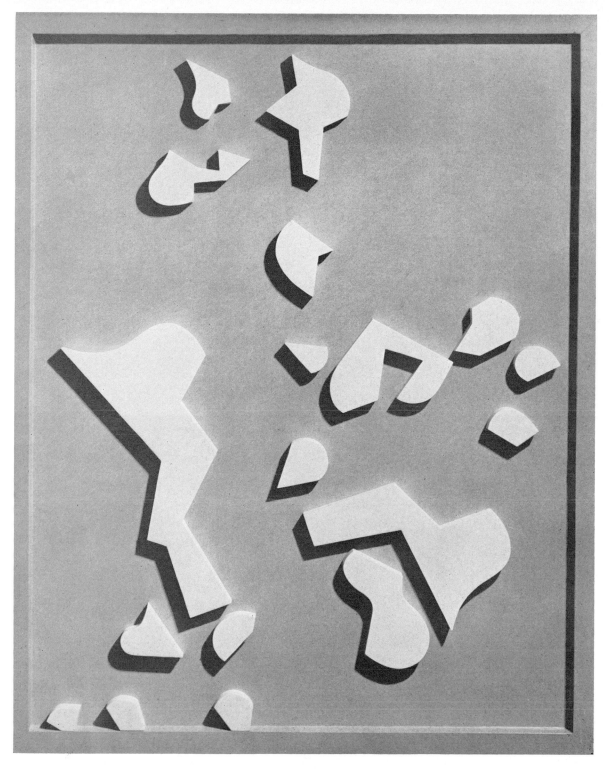

Tournament. 1949. Painted wood relief, 55 x 43½″. Sidney Janis Gallery, New York

Extremity of a Mythical Wineskin. 1952. Granite, 17″ high. The Art Institute of Chicago, Samuel P. Avery Fund

Opposite: *Pagoda Fruit.* 1949. Bronze, 43¾″ high. Galerie Springer, Berlin

Concrete Sculpture "Mirr." 1949–50. Granite, 13″ high. Private collection, New York

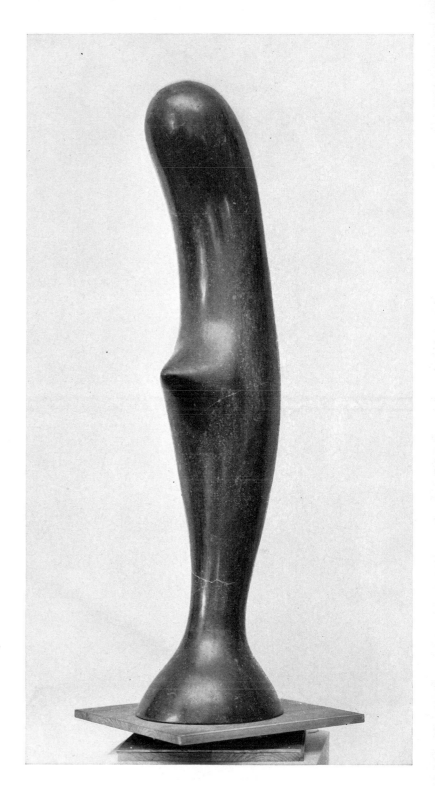

Thales of Miletus. 1951. Granite, 42″ high.
Collection Mr. and Mrs. G. David Thompson,
Pittsburgh

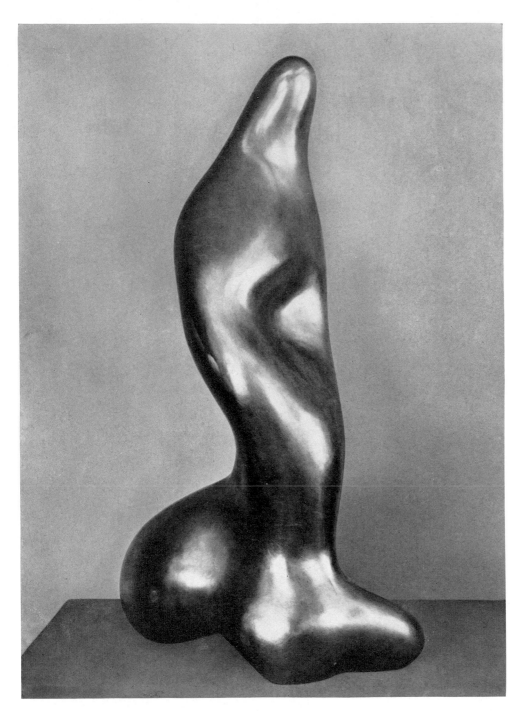

Cobra-Centaur. 1952. Bronze, 29¾″ high. Collection Mr. and Mrs. Morton G. Neumann, Chicago

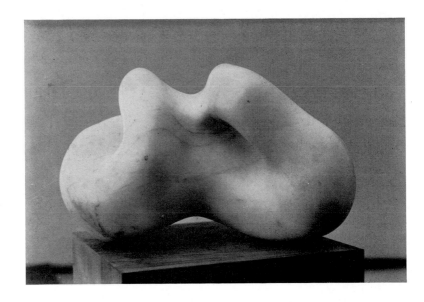

Configuration in Serpentine Movements (Snake Movement I). 1950. Marble, 14″ long. Collection Mr. and Mrs. Ralph F. Colin, New York

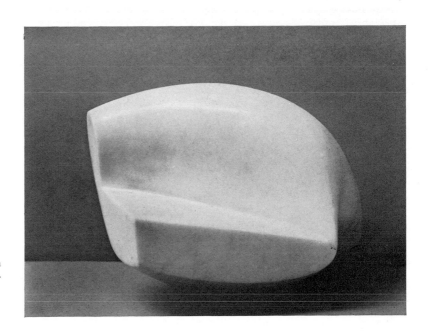

Oru. 1953. Marble, 15¾″ long. Collection Mr. and Mrs. G. David Thompson, Pittsburgh

97

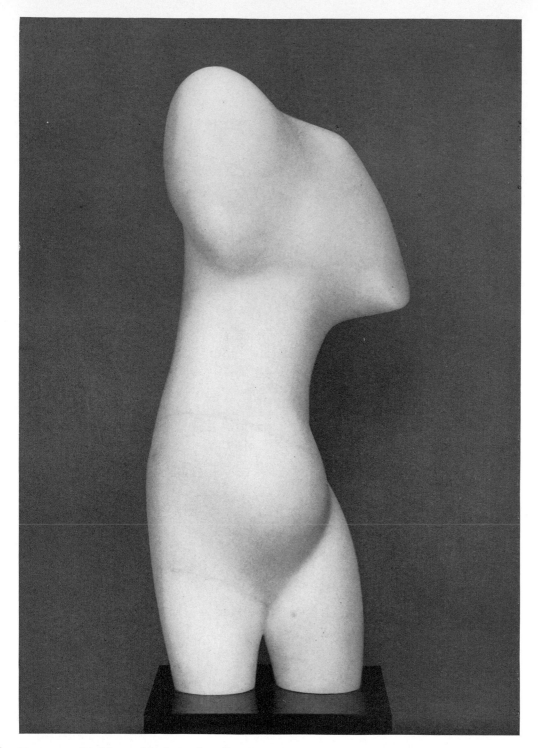

Torso. 1953. Marble, 31⅜″ high. Smith College Museum of Art, Northampton, Mass.

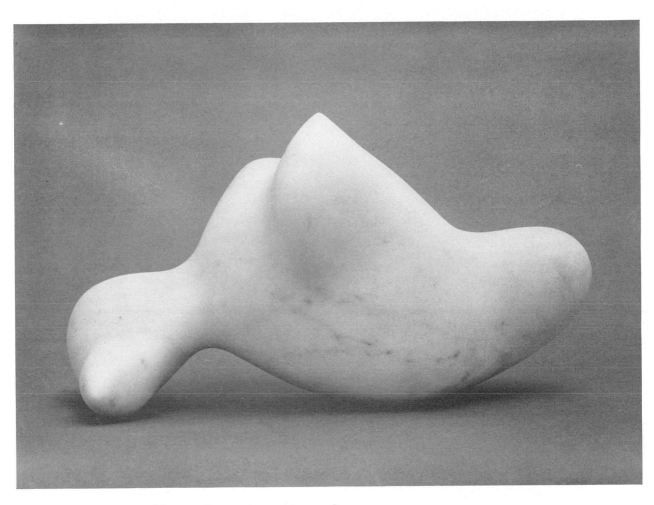

Aquatic. 1953. Marble, 25½″ long. Walker Art Center, Minneapolis

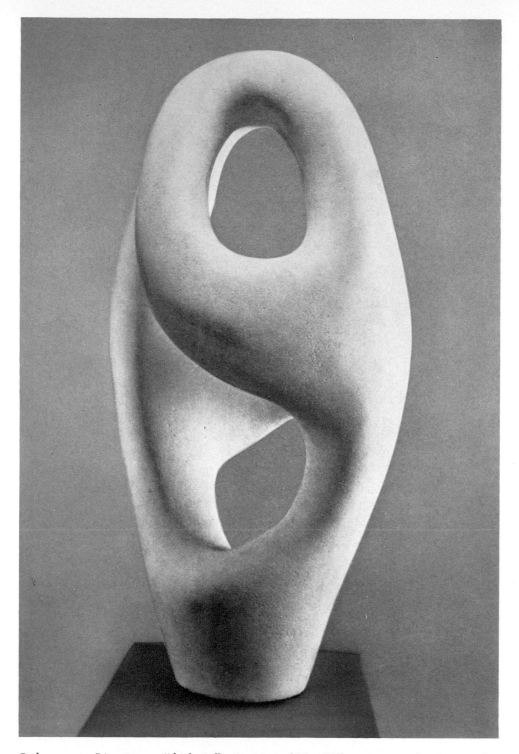

Ptolemy. 1953. Limestone, 40½ high. Collection Mr. and Mrs. William A. M. Burden, New York

Configuration: Shell-Star. 1953. Oil on cardboard, 53⅛ x 39⅜". Collection the artist

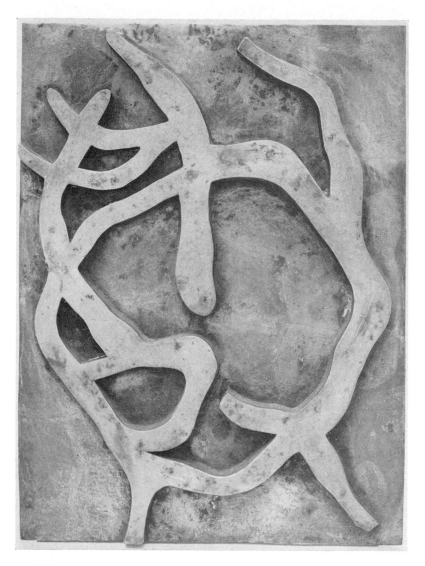

Configuration. 1955. Bronze relief, 21½ x 15¾". Collection Mr. and Mrs. Harry Jason, New York

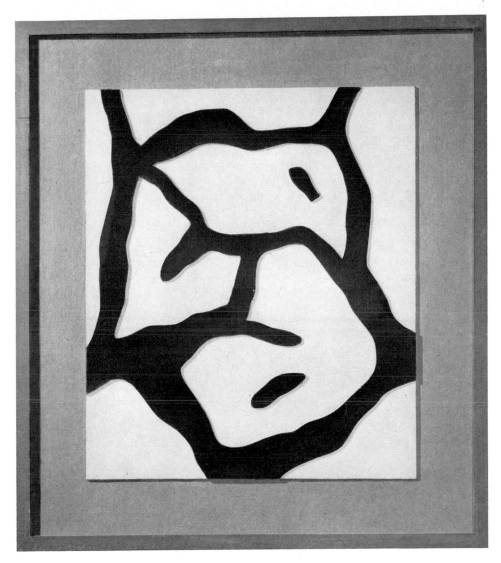

Face. 1955. Painted cardboard relief, 24⅝ x 21⅝". Collection Mme Marguerite Hagenbach, Basel

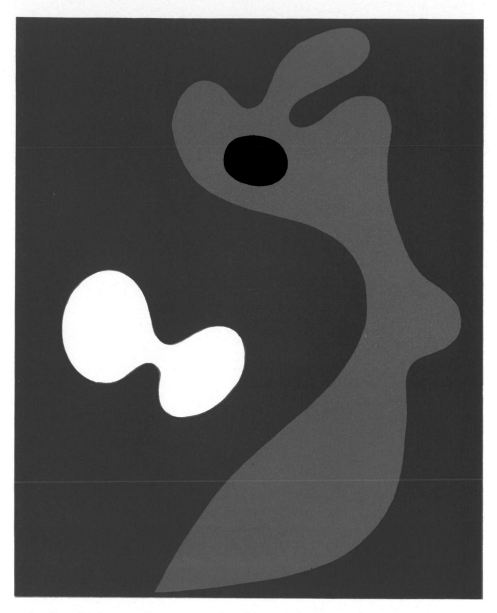

Bird and Necktie. 1954. Collage, 12¼ x 9½". Collection Mr. and Mrs. G. David Thompson, Pittsburgh

Opposite: *Dancer II.* 1955. Oil on canvas, 57⅝ x 42⅞". Collection François Arp, Paris

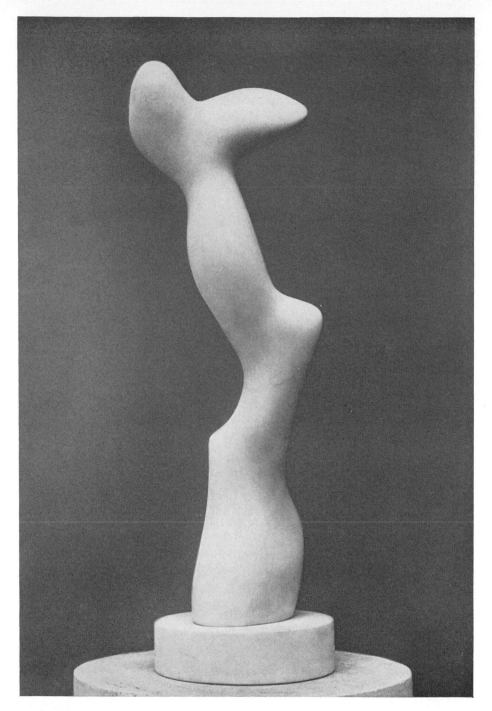

Dream Flower with Lips. 1954. Marble, 29½″ high. Collection Mrs. H. Gates Lloyd, Washington, D.C.

Right: *Mediterranean Sculpture II.* 1956. Crystallino marble, 15″ high. Collection Mme Marguerite Hagenbach, Basel

Below: *Ganymede.* 1954. Bronze, 13″ long. Collection Mr. and Mrs. Walter Bareiss, Greenwich, Conn.

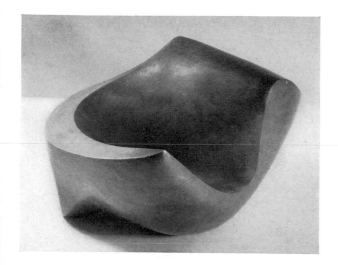

Snake Movement II. 1955. Concrete stone, 29⅛″ long. Collection Nelson A. Rockefeller, New York

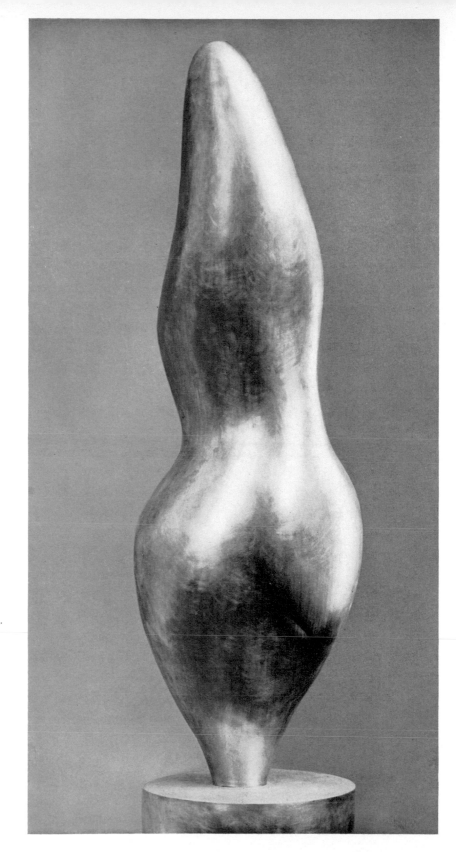

Venus of Meudon. 1956. Bronze, 62¼″ high.
Sidney Janis Gallery, New York

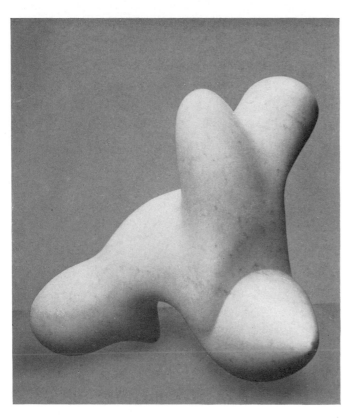

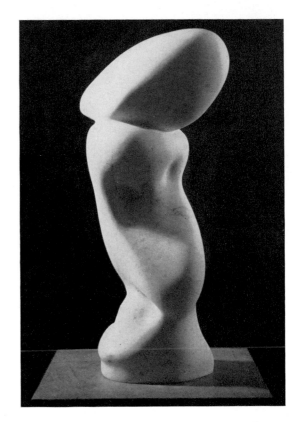

Seated. 1957. Marble, 23⅝″ high. Sidney Janis Gallery, New York

Self Absorbed. 1957. Marble, 21⅝″ high. Collection Dr. and Mrs. John Alfred Cook, New York

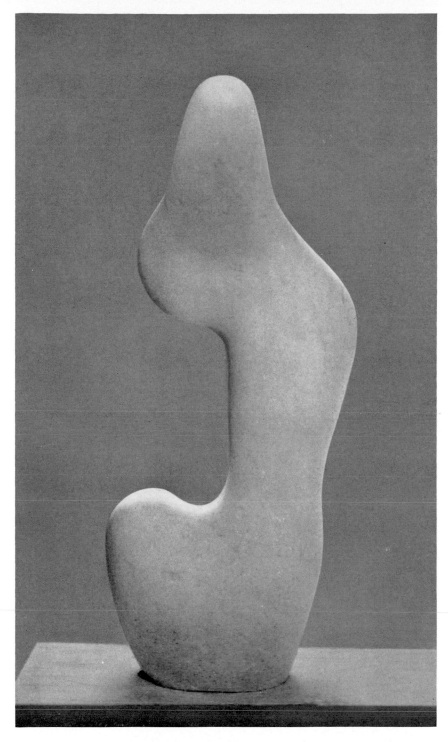

Hurlou. 1957. Marble, 38½″ high. Collection Mr. and Mrs. Boris Leavitt, Hanover, Pa.

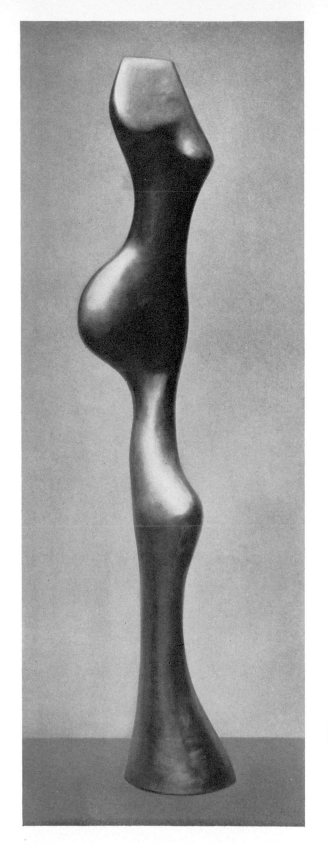

Great Lady. 1957. Bronze, 66″ high. Sidney Janis Gallery, New York

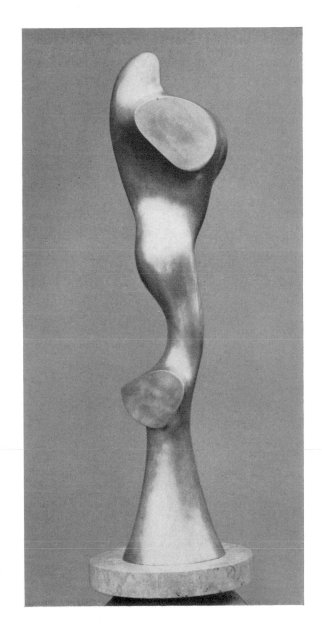

Floral Nude. 1957. Bronze, 37¼″ high.
Collection Mr. and Mrs. Charles Zadok, New York

Torso. 1957. Bronze, 36⅜″ high. Collection Mr. and Mrs. Alan Wurtzburger, courtesy The Baltimore Museum of Art

Human Lunar Spectral (Torso of a Giant). 1958. Bronze, 47¼″ high. Collection Mr. and Mrs. Burton G. Tremaine, Meriden, Conn.

Above: *Constellation of Three White Forms on Black Ground.* 1957. Collage, 27⅛ x 21⅝″. Collection the artist

Left: *Constellation of Six Black Forms on White Ground.* 1957. Collage, 43¼ x 13⅞″. Collection the artist

Opposite: *Composition in Grey, Black, and Red.* 1958. Tapestry (Ateliers Tabard, Aubusson), 60⅜ x 52⅜″. Galerie Denise René, Paris

PHOTO CREDITS

Abstract Composition. 1915. Collage, 9¼ x 7⅞". Mme Marguerite Hagenbach, Basel

118

SELECTIVE BIBLIOGRAPHY

Owing to the substantial international documentation already available in several works (bibl. 1–6), as well as the comprehensive record by Marguerite Hagenbach in a 1957 publication (bibl. 27), the references below are limited largely to material in English. In addition, the Library has on deposit a definitive bibliography (bibl. 3) for research purposes.

BERNARD KARPEL
Librarian of the Museum

BIBLIOGRAPHIES

1 BOLLIGER, HANS, ed. Begründer der moderner Plastik. p.11–12, 20–21. Zurich, Kunsthaus, 1954. *Exhibition catalogue (Nov.–Dec.), including chronology and bibliography. Also note bibl. 3, 37*

2 HAGENBACH, MARGUERITE. Documentation [on Jean Arp]. *See bibl. 27*

3 HAGENBACH, MARGUERITE & BOLLIGER, HANS, comp. [Arp bibliography]. 23 leaves [1948]. *An exhaustive list in typescript of published material in all languages up to 1948, including exhibitions. Photostatic copy in the Museum of Modern Art Library*

4 KARPEL, BERNARD. Bibliography [on Jean Arp]. *See bibl. 9, also 26, 32*

5 VERKAUF, WILLY. Dada-bibliography. *See bibl. 37*

6 VOLLMER, HANS, ed. Allgemeines Lexikon der bildenden Künstler des XX. Jahrhunderts. Vol. 1, p.69. Leipzig, Seemann, 1953.

BOOKS BY ARP

7 Dreams and projects. 15p. plus 28 pl. New York, Curt Valentin [1951–52]. *Trilingual text and original woodcuts; edition of 320 copies (25 with suite on Japan paper)*

8 The Isms of art, by El Lissitsky and Hans Arp. 11p. plus 48 pl. Erlenbach-Zurich, etc., Rentsch, 1925. *Trilingual text*

9 On my way: poetry and essays, 1912 . . . 1947. 147p. ill. New York, Wittenborn, Schultz, 1948. *Documents of modern art 6, ed. by Robert Motherwell; essays by C. Giedion-Welcker and G. Buffet-Picabia; bibliography by B. Karpel, p.135–47. Includes original texts and two original woodcuts*

ESSAYS, POEMS, INTRODUCTIONS BY ARP

10 Abstract art — concrete art. p.29–31 *In* GUGGENHEIM, PEGGY, ed. Art of This Century . . . 1910 to 1942. New York, Art of This Century, 1942. *Also p.101 (poem)*

11 [Interview: Nothing at all]. *Time* 53no.5:37–38 ill. Jan. 31, 1949.

12 [Introduction. p.3,5,7] *In* Valentin, Curt, Gallery. Jean Arp, March 2–27. New York, 1954. *Also statement in Jan.–Feb. 1949 catalogue (p.6–7)*

13 Introduction to Max Ernst's Natural History. p.124–5 *In* Max Ernst: Beyond painting. New York, Wittenborn, Schultz, 1948.

14 Kandinsky the poet. p.161 *In* Bill, Max, ed. Wassily Kandinsky. Boston, Institute of Contemporary Art; Paris, Maeght, 1951.

15 Notes from a diary. *Transition* no.21:190–4 Mar. 1932. *Also poetic extracts, no.7:130–1 Oct. 1927*

16 Pyramid frock. p.313 *In* Moholy-Nagy, L. Vision in motion. Chicago, Theobald, 1947. *Also bibl. 19*

17 Reflections of a sculptor. p.149–54 *In* American Abstract Artists, ed. The world of abstract art. New York, Wittenborn, 1957. *Replies to questions by G. L. K. Morris*

18 Serious and droll speculations. p.27–28 *In* Detroit Institute of Arts. Collecting modern art . . . the collection of Mr. and Mrs. Harry Lewis Winston. Detroit, 1957.

19 The skeleton of the day. *Transition* no.26:9–12 1937.

20 A sweet voice sings in the hump of glass. *Possibilities* no.1:16 Winter 1947–48.

21 Transformation. p.251 *In* Kepes, Gyorgy. The new landscape in art and science. Chicago, Theobald, 1956.

REFERENCES ON ARP

22 Aspects of Modern Art. p.70–81, 128–135 ill. Paris, Bernier; New York, Reynal [1957] *Selective Eye III, including essays by Seuphor on "The international dada" and "Jean Arp"*

23 Barr, Alfred H., Jr., ed. Fantastic art, dada, surrealism. Essays by Georges Hugnet. 3. ed. p.268 (index) ill. New York, Museum of Modern Art, 1947. *Published 1936, revised 1937. Includes chronology, bibliography. Also see Barr's "Cubism and Abstract Art," 1936 (p.186,204)*

24 Candee, Marjorie D., ed. Arp. *Current Biography* 15no.5:7–9 ill. May 1954. *References. Also published in "Current Biography Yearbook" (New York, Wilson, 1954)*

25 Ernst, Max [Preface]. *In* Art of This Century. Arp [exhibition catalog]. New York, [gallery imprint], 1944.

26 Giedion-Welcker, Carola. Contemporary sculpture: an evolution in volume and space. p.100–109, 302–303 et passim ill. New York, Wittenborn, 1955. *Extensive bibliography by B. Karpel. References also in her earlier publication: "Modern Plastic Art." (Zurich, Girsberger, 1937)*

27 Giedion-Welcker, Carola. Jean Arp. Documentation Marguerite Hagenbach. 122p. ill. New York, Abrams, 1957. *Bibliography, p.113–122*

28 Giedion-Welcker, Carola. Jean Arp. *Horizon* 14no. 82:232–9 ill. Oct. 1946.

29 Hess, Thomas B. Arp: well-rounded mystic. *Art News* 47no.9:20–21 ill. Jan. 1949. *Review of Arp's first Valentin show. (bibl. 36). For representative reviews see Art News 53;16–17, 55–56 Mar. 1954 (Lansner); Art Digest 29no.11:14, 24–25 Mar. 1954 (Rubin); Arts 30no.5:13 Feb. 1956 (Mellquist)*

30 Moholy-Nagy, Laslo. Vision in motion. p.313–315 et passim Chicago, Theobald, 1947. *Includes poems*

31 Morris, George L. K. Hans Arp. *Partisan Review* 4no.2:32 ill. Jan. 1937. *Critical comment also in A. E. Gallatin Collection: Museum of Living Art. p.[23] 1940. Note bibl. 16*

32 Motherwell, Robert, ed. The dada painters and poets: an anthology. p.378,382 (index) ill. New York, Wittenborn, Schultz, 1951. *Includes writings by Arp (p.221–5, 293–6), extensive references, bibliography by B. Karpel (p.317–77)*

33 Ribemont-Dessaignes, Georges. Dada painting, or the oil-eye. *Little Review* 9no.4:10–12 ill. Autumn–Winter 1923–24.

34 Seuphor, Michel. Profile of Jean Arp. *Art Digest* 28no.18:16–17 ill. July 1954. *Also preface to exhibition catalogue: "Arp" (New York, Sidney Janis Gallery, Jan.–Feb. 1950), essays in The Selective Eye (bibl. 22)*

35 Seuphor, Michel. Dictionary of modern painting. p.9–10 ill. New York, Paris Book Center [1955]. *Similarly in his Dictionary of abstract painting (1957), p.122–123*

36 Valentin, Curt, Gallery. Jean Arp [exhibitions]. v.p. ill. New York, Buchholz Gallery — Curt Valentin Gallery, 1949–1954. *First catalog (Jan.–Feb., 1949) includes "On sincerity — the work of Jean Arp" by Jean Cathelin; the second (Mar. 1954), a new text by the artist*

37 Verkauf, Willy, ed. Dada: monograph of a movement. p.34–6, 64–7, 98–100, 109–17, 141–54, 159–62, 165–73 et passim New York, Wittenborn, 1957. *Co-editors: Marcel Janco, Hans Bolliger. Trilingual text. Extensive documentation*

38 Vézelay, Paule. Jean Arp. *World Review* (n.s.) 7:61–4 ill. Sept. 1949.

LENDERS TO THE EXHIBITION

François Arp, Paris; Jean Arp, Meudon, France; Lee A. Ault, New York; Mr. and Mrs. Walter Bareiss, Greenwich, Connecticut; Mr. and Mrs. Herbert Bayer, Aspen, Colorado; Mr. and Mrs. William A. M. Burden, New York; Miss Pamela T. Colin, New York; Mr. and Mrs. Ralph F. Colin, New York; Dr. and Mrs. John Alfred Cook, New York; Oscar Cox, Washington, D.C.; Mrs. Maurice E. Culberg, Chicago; Mme Carola Giedion-Welcker, Zurich, Switzerland; Fernand C. Graindorge, Liège, Belgium; Mme Marguerite Hagenbach, Basel, Switzerland; Mr. and Mrs. George Heard Hamilton, New Haven, Connecticut; Joseph H. Hirshhorn, New York; Dr. and Mrs. Charles R. Hulbeck, New York; Mr. and Mrs. William Jaffe, New York; Sidney Janis, New York; Mr. and Mrs. Harry Jason, New York; Mr. and Mrs. Samuel M. Kootz, New York; Mr. and Mrs. Boris Leavitt, Hanover, Pennsylvania; Lucien Lefebvre-Foinet, Paris; Mrs. H. Gates Lloyd, Washington, D.C.; Mr. and Mrs. Morton D. May, St. Louis, Missouri; Mr. and Mrs. Morton G. Neumann, Chicago; Mrs. Albert H. Newman, Chicago; Roland Penrose, London; Nelson A. Rockefeller, New York; Dr. and Mrs. Israel Rosen, Baltimore, Maryland; Mr. and Mrs. Herbert M. Rothschild, Kitchawan, New York; Mr. and Mrs. Joseph Slifka, New York; Mr. and Mrs. G. David Thompson, Pittsburgh; Mr. and Mrs. Burton G. Tremaine, Meriden, Connecticut; Mr. and Mrs. Wackernagel-Hagenbach, Basel, Switzerland; Mr. and Mrs. George Henry Warren, New York; Mr. and Mrs. Richard K. Weil, St. Louis, Missouri; Mr. and Mrs. Harry L. Winston, Birmingham, Michigan; Mr. and Mrs. Alan Wurtzburger, Pikesville, Maryland; Mr. and Mrs. Charles Zadok, New York; Mr. and Mrs. Frederick Zimmermann, New York

Museum of Art, University of Michigan, Ann Arbor; The Baltimore Museum of Art, Maryland; Kunstmuseum, Basel, Switzerland; The Art Institute of Chicago, Illinois; Walker Art Center, Minneapolis, Minnesota; The Museum of Modern Art, New York; Smith College Museum of Art, Northampton, Massachusetts; Philadelphia Museum of Art, Pennsylvania; Munson-Williams-Proctor Institute, Utica, New York; Wellesley College Art Museum, Wellesley, Massachusetts

Galerie Springer, Berlin; Sidney Janis Gallery, New York; Galerie Denise René, Paris

CATALOGUE

All works in the exhibition are illustrated. In dimensions, height precedes width unless otherwise noted.

PAINTINGS, TAPESTRIES, GRAPHIC WORK

1 *Composition I.* 1907. Oil on canvas, 15¾ x 19¾″. Collection Oscar Cox, Washington, D.C. *Ill. p. 121*

2 *Crucifixion.* 1914. Engraving, 4½ x 3½″. Collection Lucien Lefebvre-Foinet, Paris. *Ill. p. 8*

3 *Horses.* 1914. Six engravings (originally executed for an unpublished de luxe edition of the Bhagavad-Gita). 9⅞ x 13″ each. Collection the artist. *Ill. p. 13*

4 *Static Composition.* 1915. Oil on cardboard, 35⅜ x 30¼″. Collection François Arp, Paris. *Ill. p. 34*

5 *Automatic Drawing.* 1916. Ink, 16¾ x 21¼″. The Museum of Modern Art, New York, given anonymously. *Ill. p. 25*

6 *Automatic Drawing.* 1918 (Original drawing for woodcut, frontispiece of *Les Feuilles Libres,* no. 47. 1927–28). Ink, 10⅝ x 8⅛″. Collection Mr. and Mrs. Morton G. Neumann, Chicago. *Ill. p. 14*

7 *The Navel Bottle.* c. 1918. Lithograph, 16⅜ x 9⅝″. The Museum of Modern Art, New York, gift of J. B. Neumann. *Ill. p. 17*

8 *Moustache Hat.* c. 1918. Lithograph, 10¾ x 13″. The Museum of Modern Art, New York, gift of J. B. Neumann. *Ill. p. 7*

9 *Abstract Composition.* 1926. Oil on canvas, 22¾ x 26″. Collection Mr. and Mrs. G. David Thompson, Pittsburgh. *Ill. p. 47*

10 *Navels.* 1926. Oil on canvas, 19¾ x 23⅝″. Collection Mme Marguerite Hagenbach, Basel. *Ill. p. 46*

11 Rug. 1938. Wool, 78 x 59½″. The Museum of Modern Art, New York. Purchase. *Ill. p. 67*

12 *Dancer II.* 1955 (painting after *Dancer I,* 1928, destroyed relief). Oil on canvas, 57⅝ x 42⅞″. Collection François Arp, Paris. *Ill. p. 105*

13 *Planimetric Sculpture.* 1958. Pencil, 27½ x 19¾″. Collection the artist. *Ill. p. 10*

14 *Composition in Grey, Black, and Red.* 1958. Tapestry (Ateliers Tabard, Aubusson), 60⅝ x 52⅜″. Galerie Denise René, Paris. *Ill. p. 117*

15 *Skeleton and Moustache.* 1958. Tapestry (Ateliers Tabard, Aubusson), 59⅞ x 49¼″. Galerie Denise René, Paris. *Illustrated on jacket*

COLLAGES

16 *Abstract Composition.* 1915. Collage, 9¼ x 7⅞". Collection Mme Marguerite Hagenbach, Basel. *Ill. p. 118*

17 *Rectangles Arranged According to the Laws of Chance.* 1916. Collage, 9⅞ x 4⅞". Collection the artist. *Ill. p. 35*

18 *Squares Arranged According to the Laws of Chance.* 1916–17. Collage, 19⅛ x 13⅝". The Museum of Modern Art, New York. Purchase. *Ill. p. 37*

19 *Duo-Collage.* 1918 (Executed in collaboration with Sophie Taeuber-Arp). Paper on cardboard, 33⅞ x 26". Collection Mr. and Mrs. Burton G. Tremaine, Meriden, Conn. *Ill. p. 37*

20 *Papier Déchiré.* 1932. Collage, 17⅛ x 14¾". Collection the artist. *Ill. p. 15*

21 *Torn Drawing.* 1932. Collage, 20⅞ x 18⅛". Collection the artist. *Ill. p. 60*

22 *Navel and Winged Navel.* 1933. Collage, 15¾ x 13½". Collection François Arp, Paris. *Ill. p. 60*

23 *Composition.* 1937. Torn paper, with India ink wash, 11½ x 12¾". Philadelphia Museum of Art, A. E. Gallatin Collection. *Ill. p. 66*

24 *Composition.* 1937. Torn paper, with India ink wash and pencil, 11¾ x 9". Philadelphia Museum of Art, A. E. Gallatin Collection. *Ill. p. 66*

25 *Torn Drawing with Watercolor.* 1946. Collage, 13¾ x 9¾". Collection Mme Marguerite Hagenbach, Basel. *Ill. p. 82*

26 *Drawing and Torn and Colored Papers.* 1946. Collage, 13¾ x 9⅞". Collection Mr. and Mrs. Wackernagel-Hagenbach, Basel. *Ill. p. 82*

27 *Color Tear.* 1947. Collage and gouache, 24¾ x 19". Collection Mr. and Mrs. William Jaffe, New York. *Ill. p. 83*

28 *Personage.* 1948. Collage and gouache, 19¼ x 10⅞". Wellesley College Art Museum, gift of Edgar Kaufmann, Wellesley, Mass. *Ill. p. 88*

29 *In the Manner of Papiers Déchirés.* 1949. Collage, 14¾ x 12⅞". Collection Dr. and Mrs. Charles R. Hulbeck, New York. *Ill. p. 90*

30 *Bird and Necktie.* 1954. Collage, 12¼ x 9½". Collection Mr. and Mrs. G. David Thompson, Pittsburgh. *Ill. p. 104*

31 *Constellation of Six Black Forms on White Ground.* 1957. Collage, 43¼ x 13⅞". Collection the artist. *Ill. p. 116*

32 *Constellation of Three White Forms on Black Ground.* 1957. Collage, 27⅛ x 21⅝". Collection the artist. *Ill. p. 116*

Composition I. 1907. Oil on canvas, 15¾ x 19¾". Oscar Cox, Washington, D.C.

RELIEFS

33 *Portrait of Tzara.* 1916. Painted wood relief, 18⅞ x 18¼" Collection the artist. *Ill. p. 19*

34 *Forest.* 1916. Painted wood relief, 12⅞ x 7½". Collection Roland Penrose, London. *Ill. p. 35*

35 *Plant Hammer.* 1917. Painted wood relief, 24¾ x 19⅝". Collection the artist. *Ill. p. 36*

36 *Birds in an Aquarium.* c. 1920. Painted wood, 9⅞ x 8". The Museum of Modern Art, New York. *Ill. p. 38*

37 *Shirt Front and Fork.* 1922. Painted wood, 22 x 27½". Collection Mr. and Mrs. George Heard Hamilton, New Haven, Conn. *Ill. p. 38*

38 *Egg Board.* 1922. Painted wood, 29½ x 39". Collection Fernand C. Graindorge, Liège, Belgium. *Ill. p. 39*

39 *Plate, Fork, and Navel.* 1923. Painted wood relief, 23¼ x 24". Sidney Janis Gallery, New York. *Ill. p. 41*

40 *Dancer.* 1923–24. String and oil on canvas, 20 x 15¾". Sidney Janis Gallery, New York. *Ill. p. 40*

41 *Moon Frog.* 1924. Oil on cardboard with cut-outs, 20½ x 27½". Collection Mme Marguerite Hagenbach, Basel. *Ill. p. 42*

42 *Mountain, Table, Anchors, Navel.* 1925. Oil on cardboard with cut-outs, 29⅝ x 23½". The Museum of Modern Art, New York. Purchase. *Ill. p. 43*

43 *Shirt and Tie.* 1928. Painted wood relief, 31⅜ x 39⅜". Private collection, New York. *Ill. p. 48*

44 *Two Heads.* 1929. Painted wood relief, 47¼ x 39¼". The Museum of Modern Art, New York. Purchase. *Ill. p. 53*

45 *Leaf.* 1929. Oil and string on canvas, 28¾ x 23½". Private collection, New York. *Ill. p. 50*

46 *Leaves and Navels.* 1929. Oil and string on canvas, 13¾ x 10¾". The Museum of Modern Art, New York. *Ill. p. 51*

47 *Arranged According to the Laws of Chance.* 1929. Painted wood relief, 55⅛ x 42⅛". Private collection, Switzerland. *Ill. p. 49*

48 *Objects Arranged According to the Laws of Chance or Navels.* 1930. Varnished wood relief, 10⅝ x 11⅛". The Museum of Modern Art, New York. Purchase. *Ill. p. 51*

49 *Leaves and Navels I.* 1930. Painted wood relief, 31¾ x 39¾". The Museum of Modern Art, New York. Purchase. *Ill. p. 56*

50 *Torso, Navel, Head with Moustache.* 1930. Painted wood relief, 31½ x 39¼". Collection Mrs. Albert H. Newman, Chicago. *Ill. p. 52*

51 *Configuration.* 1930. Painted wood relief, 27½ x 33½". Philadelphia Museum of Art, A. E. Gallatin Collection. *Ill. p. 57*

52 *Variation I — Constellation with Five White and Two Black Forms.* 1932. Painted wood relief, 23½ x 29½". Munson-Williams-Proctor Institute, Utica, N.Y. *Ill. p. 59*

53 *Arrow Cloud.* 1932. Painted wood relief, 43¼ x 55⅛". Private collection, Basel. *Ill. p. 58*

54 *Construction.* 1934. Oil on board with cut-outs, 28½ x 40". Collection Mr. and Mrs. Herbert M. Rothschild, Kitchawan, New York. *Ill. p. 61*

55 *Three Constellations of Same Forms.* 1942. Painted wood reliefs, 35¾ x 28" each. Private collection, Basel. *Ill. pp. 76, 77*

56 *Birdlike Cloud.* 1943. Painted wood relief, 32½ x 28". Collection Dr. and Mrs. Charles R. Hulbeck, New York. *Ill. p. 78*

57 *Structure of White Blossoms for My Dead Wife.* 1943. Painted wood relief, 55⅛ x 43¾". Collection Mme Marguerite Hagenbach, Basel. *Ill. p. 79*

58 *Vegetal Symmetry.* 1946. Wood relief, 21⅝ x 19¼". Collection Mme Carola Giedion-Welcker, Zurich. *Ill. p. 80*

59 *Summer Metope.* 1946. Wood relief, 55⅞ x 25⅝". Collection the artist. *Ill. p. 81*

60 *Star Seed.* 1949. Painted wood, 17½ x 24½". Collection Mrs. Maurice E. Culberg, Chicago. *Ill. p. 90*

61 *Tournament.* 1949. Painted wood relief, 55 x 43½". Sidney Janis Gallery, New York. *Ill. p. 91*

62 *Configuration: Shell-Star.* 1953. Oil on cardboard, 53⅛ x 39⅜". Collection the artist. *Ill. p. 101*

63 *Configuration.* 1955. Bronze relief, 21½ x 15¾". Collection Mr. and Mrs. Harry Jason, New York. *Ill. p. 102*

64 *Face.* 1955. Painted cardboard relief, 24⅝ x 21⅝". Collection Mme Marguerite Hagenbach, Basel. *Ill. p. 103*

SCULPTURE

The dating and dimensions of the sculpture section are largely based on the catalogue of Arp's sculpture by Marguerite Hagenbach in Jean Arp *by Carola Giedion-Welcker, 1957, published by Harry N. Abrams, Inc., New York. Several additions and changes have been made in view of more recent information.*

65 *Hand Fruit.* 1930. Painted wood, 21⅝ x 34⅝". Private collection, Switzerland. *Ill. p. 54*

66 *Bell and Navels.* 1931. Painted wood, 10¼ x 19¼". Collection the artist. *Ill. p. 55*

67 *To be Lost in the Woods.* 1932. Bronze sculpture in three forms: large, 8¾" long; medium, 4¾" long; small, 3⅝" long. Base: 24" high. Collection Sidney Janis, New York. *Ill. p. 55*

68 *Human Concretion on Oval Bowl.* 1935. Bronze. Sculpture, 18¼" high; bowl, 28⅜" long. Collection the artist. *Ill. p. 63*

69 *Human Concretion.* 1935. Cast stone (1949, after original plaster), 19½" high. The Museum of Modern Art, New York, gift of the Advisory Committee. *Ill. p. 65*

70 *Metamorphosis (Shell-Swan-Swing).* 1935. Bronze, 27⅛" high (Derived from original plaster, 1935, 9" high). Collection the artist. *Ill. p. 62*

71 *Crown of Buds.* 1936. Bronze (1947, after original limestone), 18½" high. Collection Mr. and Mrs. Samuel M. Kootz, New York. *Ill. p. 68*

72 *Marital Sculpture.* 1937. Wood (lathe-turned and sawed, executed in collaboration with Sophie Taeuber-Arp), 15⅜" high. Collection the artist. *Ill. p. 64*

73 *Stone Formed by the Human Hand.* 1938. Jura limestone, 16¼" high. Kunstmuseum, Basel, Emanuel Hoffmann Fund. *Ill. p. 71*

74 *Automatic Sculpture (Homage to Rodin).* 1938. Granite, 10¼" high. Collection Mr. and Mrs. Richard K. Weil, St. Louis. *Ill. p. 68*

75 *Awakening.* 1938. Bronze (1958, after original plaster), 18⅝" high. Collection Mr. and Mrs. Joseph Slifka, New York. *Ill. p. 72*

76 *Growth.* 1938. Bronze, 31½" high. Philadelphia Museum of Art. *Ill. p. 69*

77 *Lunar Armor.* 1938. Granite, 15" high. Collection Mr. and Mrs. Harry L. Winston, Birmingham, Mich. *Ill. p. 70*

78 *Pre-Adamic Fruit.* 1938. Bronze, 11¼″ high. Museum of Art, University of Michigan, Ann Arbor. *Ill. p. 72*

79 *Shell Crystal.* 1938. Granite, 13″ high. Collection Nelson A. Rockefeller, New York. *Ill. p. 73*

80 *Pre-Adamic Torso.* 1938. Limestone, 18⅞″ high. Collection Mme Marguerite Hagenbach, Basel. *Ill. p. 70*

81 *Leaf of the Pyramids.* 1939. Granite, 18″ long. The Baltimore Museum of Art, Charles and Elsa Hutzler Memorial Collection. *Ill. p. 73*

82 *Dream Amphora.* 1941. Marble, 9″ high. Collection Mr. and Mrs. Herbert Bayer, Aspen, Colorado. *Ill. p. 75*

83 *Concrete Sculpture.* 1942. Marble, 14⅛″ high. Collection Miss Pamela T. Colin, New York, courtesy Mr. and Mrs. Ralph F. Colin. *Ill. p. 74*

84 *Little Sphinx.* 1942. Bronze, 16⅛″ high. Collection Mr. and Mrs. Joseph Slifka, New York. *Ill. p. 74*

85 *Snake Bread.* 1942. Granite, 10¼″ long. Collection Mr. and Mrs. Frederick Zimmermann, New York. *Ill. p. 75*

86 *Chimerical Font.* 1947. Bronze, 31½″ high. Collection Mr. and Mrs. George Henry Warren, New York. *Ill. p. 85*

87 *Owl's Dream.* 1947. Marble, 15¾″ high. (Derived from original limestone, 1937–38, 10¼″ high). Collection Lee A. Ault, New York. *Ill. p. 87*

88 *Tree of Bowls.* 1947. Bronze, 39⅜″ high. Collection Mr. and Mrs. Richard K. Weil, St. Louis. *Ill. p. 84*

89 *Head with Claws.* 1949. Bronze, 18½″ high. Collection Joseph H. Hirshhorn, New York. *Ill. p. 86*

90 *Pagoda Fruit.* 1949. Bronze, 43¾″ high. (Derived from cast cement, 1934, 9″ high). Galerie Springer, Berlin. *Ill. p. 92*

91 *Silent.* 1949. Marble, 20″ high. (Derived from original plaster, 1942, 13⅜″ high). Collection Dr. and Mrs. Israel Rosen, Baltimore. *Ill. p. 86*

92 *Concrete Sculpture "Mirr."* 1949–50. Granite, 13″ high. (Derived from bronze, 1936, 5⅞″ high). Private collection, New York. *Ill. p. 94*

93 *Pistil.* 1950. Limestone, 34⅝″ high. (Derived from limestone, 1950, 13⅜″ high). Collection Mr. and Mrs. Morton D. May, St. Louis. *Ill. p. 89*

94 *Configuration in Serpentine Movements (Snake Movement I).* 1950. Marble, 14″ long. Collection Mr. and Mrs. Ralph F. Colin, New York. *Ill. p. 97*

95 *Thales of Miletus.* 1951. Granite, 42″ high. Collection Mr. and Mrs. G. David Thompson, Pittsburgh. *Ill. p. 95*

96 *Extremity of a Mythical Wineskin.* 1952. Granite, 17″ high. The Art Institute of Chicago, Samuel P. Avery Fund. *Ill. p. 93*

97 *Cobra-Centaur.* 1952. Bronze, 29¾″ high. Collection Mr. and Mrs. Morton G. Neumann, Chicago. *Ill. p. 96*

98 *Torso.* 1953. Marble, 31⅜″ high. (Derived from original plaster, 1930, 12¼″ high). Smith College Museum of Art, Northampton, Mass. *Ill. p. 98*

99 *Oru.* 1953. Marble, 15¾″ long. Collection Mr. and Mrs. G. David Thompson, Pittsburgh. *Ill. p. 97*

100 *Aquatic.* 1953. Marble, 25½″ long. Walker Art Center, Minneapolis. *Ill. p. 99*

101 *Ptolemy.* 1953. Limestone, 40½″ high. Collection Mr. and Mrs. William A. M. Burden, New York. *Ill. p. 100*

102 *Ganymede.* 1954. Bronze, 13″ long. (Derived from *Shell*, 1938, 4¾″ high). Collection Mr. and Mrs. Walter Bareiss, Greenwich, Conn. *Ill. p. 107*

103 *Dream Flower with Lips.* 1954. Marble, 29½″ high. (Derived from original plaster, 1954, 18⅛″ high). Collection Mrs. H. Gates Lloyd, Washington, D.C. *Ill. p. 106*

104 *Snake Movement II.* 1955. Concrete stone, 29⅛″ long. (Derived from limestone, 1955, 13⅜″ long). Collection Nelson A. Rockefeller, New York. *Ill. p. 108*

105 *Mediterranean Sculpture II.* 1956. Crystallino marble, 15″ high. (Derived from white marble, 1942, 14¾″ high). Mme Marguerite Hagenbach, Basel. *Ill. p. 107*

106 *Venus of Meudon.* 1956. Bronze, 62¼″ high. Sidney Janis Gallery, New York. *Ill. p. 109*

107 *Self Absorbed.* 1957. Marble, 21⅝″ high. (Derived from limestone, 1956, 21⅝″ high). Collection Dr. and Mrs. John Alfred Cook, New York. *Ill. p. 110*

108 *Hurlou.* 1957. Marble, 38½″ high. (Derived from limestone, 1951, 19⅝″ high). Collection Mr. and Mrs. Boris Leavitt, Hanover, Pa. *Ill. p. 111*

109 *Floral Nude.* 1957. Bronze, 37¼″ high. Collection Mr. and Mrs. Charles Zadok, New York. *Ill. p. 113*

110 *Seated.* 1957. Marble, 23⅝″ high. (Derived from limestone, 1937, 13″ high). Sidney Janis Gallery, New York. *Ill. p. 110*

111 *Torso.* 1957. Bronze, 36⅝″ high. (Derived from marble, 1931, 24″ high). Collection Mr. and Mrs. Alan Wurtzburger, courtesy The Baltimore Museum of Art. *Ill. p. 114*

112 *Great Lady.* 1957. Bronze, 66″ high. Sidney Janis Gallery, New York. *Ill. p. 112*

113 *Human Lunar Spectral (Torso of a Giant).* 1957. Bronze, 47¼″ high. (Derived from marble, 1950, 36⅝″ high). Collection Mr. and Mrs. Burton G. Tremaine, Meriden, Conn. *Ill. p. 115*

INDEX

by Ernest Priest

Page numbers marked with an asterisk denote illustrations

This book has been printed in September 1958 for the Trustees of the Museum of Modern Art by Connecticut Printers, Inc., Hartford